Prosperity on God's Terms

Prosperity on God's Terms

by
Dr. Frederick K.C. Price

Harrison House
Tulsa, Oklahoma

Unless otherwise indicated, all Scripture quotations are taken from the *King James Version* of the Bible.

3rd Printing
Over 25,000 in Print

Prosperity on God's Terms
ISBN 0-89274-670-X
Copyright © 1990 by Dr. Frederick K.C. Price
Crenshaw Christian Center
P.O. Box 90000
Los Angeles, California 90009

Published by **Harrison House, Inc.**
P.O. Box 35035
Tulsa, Oklahoma 74153

Contents

Introduction

There are many people who live clean and moral lives that are beyond reproach! *But they are whipped, defeated, sick, poor and unable to pay their bills.* While Christianity most definitely needs positive role models from a *moral* standpoint, it also most definitely needs role models of those who have gained victory in their lives from a material standpoint as well — *but who have gained this victory by doing it God's way!*

I am convinced that if people do not see these examples of successful, prosperous Christians, they will continue to pattern their lives after men and women in the world who have used its system to gain financial independence.

Unfortunately, there are many Christians who wear poverty and lack of material prosperity as a badge of holiness. They consider their lack of this world's goods as a criterion for spirituality, when, in fact, the Bible does not support this hypothesis at all.

Most Christians are taught from the pulpit that they will receive their blessings, material and otherwise, on the "other side." So they continue to reject the goods of this life that, according to the Bible, God wants to provide for them. They have, regrettably, been listening to false teachers, and obviously have not taken the time to read and study the Bible for themselves. Because if they had, they would know that God wants to bless them in every area of this life now — not just in the "sweet bye and bye."

The devil has made a concerted effort to infiltrate the Christian community through incorrect teaching — teaching that is inconsistent with the Word of God, but which is rather consistent with the status quo of this world's system. This erroneous teaching is based on experience, and not on the Bible. Christians have to understand that in order to do *God's work* here on this earth, *it takes the possession and right use of material things!* The Bible is full of the word on *prosperity* — full of God's material *blessings being showered upon those who have been and are willing to be obedient to His Word because they love and honor Him!*

I believe this poverty syndrome that has plagued the Christian environment for so long is a diabolical plot, hatched by Satan himself, to prevent the spread of the Gospel.

Why else would the average believer want to deny the validity of that part of the Gospel message that addresses the issue of prosperity, when the Bible is so full of information on prosperity for God's people?

It has to be satanic deception for the Christian to speak against prosperity. Satan very well knows that if we become financially independent of our circumstances, he will no longer control our progress. "Poor-mouthing" Christians are not going to be very credible witnesses of the goodness of God, nor will they influence very many people. But more importantly, they are not going to get the Gospel out. They are aiding the enemy — while rejecting the command of

God Who told us to promote the Gospel — and they don't even know it.

If anybody in the world needs money, it is *those in the Kingdom of God!* There is no shortage of money in the world's financial structure; however, when Satan gains complete control of the wealth of the earth, the Gospel of our Lord and Savior will be totally hindered from getting to the masses.

Can't you see the clever scheme of the adversary?

We are God's tools in this realm, and unfortunately, He is limited by His tools. We Christians have to get into a position where we can function as powerful tools in the hands of God. What's so beautiful about doing it God's way is that in the process of being obedient to His will, all of our own needs are taken care of as well. But because most Christians are so busy just barely making it, they can't focus in on the things of God.

It is clear that God wants His children to prosper. *How can anyone deny that?* I certainly believe and agree that prosperity should not be an end in itself, but rather it ought to be the result of a quality of life, commitment, dedication and acting in line with God's Word — that's what ultimately produces the prosperity. But neither can we deny that, according to the Bible, it is God's wish that we prosper and be in health, even as our souls prosper. (3 John 2.) That verse is talking about *material* and *spiritual* prosperity! God doesn't want us to be out of balance and prosper in one area more than another.

9

I realize that the Bible says in Luke 12:15 that a person's life does not consist in the abundance of the things which he possesses. However, I also believe that the Bible promotes the fact that God wants His children to enjoy a full, total, complete style of life. He has made provision through His Word for us to be fulfilled in this life. Not only has He said that He will supply our every need, He also wants to fulfill our hearts' desires. All He requires of us is that we put our priorities in the right order. Matthew 6:33 hits the nail right on the head: **But seek ye first the kingdom of God, and his righteousness; and all these things shall be *added* unto you.**

God's will (His covenant) is for us to have life and to have it more abundantly — *not just life, but abundant life!* (John 10:10.) It is clear that the abundant life is available to us, if we will only take God at His Word!

There is really no way we can lose by following the Word, and being obedient to God and diligent to do His will. By following the directions given in the Bible, we automatically bring upon ourselves the blessings of God, which include prosperity.

Prosperity — spiritual, physical and material — is part and parcel of the Gospel message! Christians should rejoice in this fact, because through our prosperity, Satan loses! Our wealth makes it possible to spread the Good News — and that really is "the bottom line" of it all!

1

Is Prosperity God's Will?

One of my ministerial assignments from God is to teach His Word in simple, direct, layman's terms so that anyone from anywhere with an open heart and mind can hear, learn and profit thereby. Do you know that God has His specialists, just as there are specialists in various other fields of human endeavor?

Take the field of medicine, for example. There are many, many specialists in this area. There are specialists for just about every part of the body, and then some. In other fields, there are engineering specialists, agricultural specialists, industrial specialists, and even tree specialists. According to the dictionary, a specialist is one who concentrates in a particular field of study, professional work, etc.

You can call me God's prosperity specialist!

Faith, healing, the Holy Spirit, and, of course, prosperity are areas in which the Lord has led me to concentrate my teaching ministry. In this book, however, I will be primarily dealing with those issues concerning the material aspects of prosperity as it relates to the Christian community and the spread of the Gospel.

Christians are God's tools on this earth. But because most believers are so caught up in the struggles

11

of daily living, they are unable to concentrate fully on the things of God; therefore, the powerful message of the Gospel has been hampered.

The majority of believers today are handicapped by their own poverty, most of which is caused by their disobedience to the Word of God. And how are they being disobedient? There are, of course, many ways. One of the primary ways is that they are robbing God! Yes, I said *robbing God*. How? By withholding their tithes and offerings, they are stealing from the *source of all life!* As a consequence, they are robbing themselves of the blessings God wants to bestow upon them.

Tithes and Offerings

Will a man rob God? Yet ye have robbed me. But ye say, Wherein have we robbed thee? In tithes and offerings.

Ye are cursed with a curse: for ye have robbed me, even this whole nation.

Bring ye all the tithes into the storehouse, that there may be meat in mine house, and prove me now herewith, saith the Lord of hosts, if I will not open you the windows of heaven, and pour you out a blessing, that there shall not be room enough to receive it.

Malachi 3:8-10

Not only are some people not tithing, they are not even giving offerings. So they are robbing God. When you rob God, you are breaking a spiritual law. When you break a law, then that law cannot work on your behalf. If you obey God's commands, He will bless you materially and financially beyond your wildest dreams

— that is, if your main desire is to please Him and not just to get something in return.

Nobody could ever talk me out of tithing or out of giving. Although as Christians we basically tithe and give offerings to be obedient to the Lord, *He does reward obedience,* and we can expect a return!

Giving and Receiving

The more you give, the more you receive,. The Bible tells us in Acts 20:35: **...It is more blessed to give than to receive.** It is clear why this is so. The more you give, the more you will automatically receive, because then your seed sown is always multiplied. You can surely see this in the natural: If you simply plant one fruit tree seed, when the tree grows to maturity, you will have an abundance of fruit on that tree as a result of planting only one seed.

The Word tells us in Luke 6:38: **Give, and it shall be given unto you; good measure, pressed down, and shaken together, and running over, shall men give into your bosom. For with the same measure that ye mete withal, it shall be measured to you again.**

Many people want something for nothing when it comes to the things of God. And they want it right away. Yet in the world, they know that things don't work that way. Most people have enough sense to know that if they go to their local bank, they are not going to get any interests or dividends if they don't have any money invested in that bank. Yet they always expect God to send them something when they haven't invested in His Kingdom.

If you are not investing your time, talent, commitment, or money, why do you expect anything? Yet, some people even return to a life of sin because they think they're not getting anything out of the Christian life. *How can you get anything when you haven't planted or invested?* How can you expect God to honor your desire, when you haven't honored His command to give?

The Law of Divine Reciprocity

There is a universal law of divine reciprocity. You plant a seed, the ground gives you a harvest. That's a reciprocal relationship. The ground can only give to you as you give to the ground. You put money in a bank, into an interest-bearing account, and the bank gives you interest. That's reciprocity. The whole Word of God is based upon this law of reciprocity.

Notice that Luke 6:38 says to give and that it shall be returned to you, *". . . good measure, pressed down, and shaken together, and running over. . . ."* That means that you will have an abundance — that means that you will have more than enough.

Second Corinthians 9:6 states: **. . . He which soweth sparingly shall reap also sparingly; and he which soweth bountifully shall reap also bountifully.** Matthew 7:1 says: **Judge not, that ye be not judged.** Matthew 7:7 declares: **Ask, and it shall be given you; seek, and ye shall find; knock, and it shall be opened unto you.** The Bible does not say, *"Receive,* and then *ask!"* It does not say, *"Receive,* and then *give!"* No! It says, *"Give,* and you shall *receive!"* It is also implied that, if you don't ask, you won't get. If you don't seek, you won't find.

If you don't plant, you won't get a harvest!

God's Will Is Abundance

God's will is that we prosper: spirit, soul and body.

Third John 2 says: **Beloved, I wish above all things that thou mayest prosper and be in health, even as thy soul prospereth.** It is very clear from this verse that God wants us to prosper in every area of life. This scripture is not limited just to the person to whom this letter from John was addressed when he wrote, **The elder unto the wellbeloved Gaius...**(v. 1).

I believe the Spirit of God had this biblical book incorporated into the canon of scriptures because what John was saying to Gaius, the Lord is saying to everyone. The Bible tells us that ...**God is no respecter of persons** (Acts 10:34). Consequently, He could not want Gaius to prosper, but the rest of us to live in poverty. That would not make sense. I believe that 3 John 2 applies to the whole of Christendom. Jesus said, ...**According to your faith be it unto you...**(Matt. 9:29). My faith says that this scripture is speaking to me. You need to believe that it is speaking to you too, if you want to get your thinking in line with the Word of God.

There are three aspects of this verse which pertain to our betterment: 1) "...prosper...," 2) "...be in health," and 3) "even as thy soul prospereth."

Soul prosperity has to do with the spiritual areas of our lives. The "to be in health" covers our physical

15

well being. The word "prosper" refers to the material aspect of our existence.

The soul is not the body, and the body is not the soul; however, the spirit and the soul go hand in hand. Although we separate the soul and the spirit when we talk about them so that we can understand their functions, in reality, they cannot be separated. If you get the water, you get the wetness; and so it is with the spirit and the soul. However, the soul and the spirit can be separated from the body. In fact, that is exactly what happens at physical death. The soul doesn't stay in the ground with the body while the spirit departs — no, the body stays in the grave, and the soul and spirit go together to heaven.

Man is a spirit; he has a soul; and he lives inside a physical body. With each of these three component parts, he is able to contact a different realm of life. With the body, through the physical senses, he contacts the three-dimensional material world. Through his soul, which contains the desires, will, emotions and intellect, he contacts the realm of the mind and emotions. Then with the spirit he contacts God.

When a person is born again, it is the spirit which experiences new birth. The soul and body remain unchanged. It is the desire of God that the spirit of man utilize His Word to bring influence upon the soul so that the soul in turn can bring influence upon the physical body. That's why Paul wrote in Romans 12:1,2:

I beseech you therefore, brethren, by the mercies of God, that ye present your bodies a living sacrifice, holy, acceptable unto God, which is your reasonable service.

And be not conformed to this world, but be ye transformed by the renewing of your mind....

The mind is contained in the soul realm. The Apostle Paul doesn't tell us to be renewed in our spirits, because our spirits cannot be renewed; they must be *born again.* To be "born again" means to start over. When a person is born again, he becomes a brand new person. He gets a new life. Birth produces life. To *renew* something is to take it and "spruce it up." When you renew a house, for example, you paint it, wallpaper it, take out a window and put in a door, etc. What you are doing is working with the same basic building you had in the first place to restore it to its original condition.

Oppositions to Prosperity

There is a challenge to this subject of *prosperity.* There are some who openly speak against it, and there are others who very subtly attempt to undermine it. Yet the Bible is full of *prosperity!*

One of the most celebrated passages of scripture known to man is the 23rd Psalm. Folks who are not even saved can quote this psalm which begins, **The Lord is my shepherd...** (v. 1). Toward the end of this beautiful, poetic psalm, the writer states: **Thou preparest a table before me in the presence of mine enemies: thou anointest my head with oil; my cup runneth over** (v. 5).

Notice: "...*my cup runneth over.*" If that's not prosperity, I don't know what is! David didn't talk about having just a little bit — down at the bottom. He said that his cup was overflowing. If he had said, "Well, I have enough for one swig; I've got enough in my cup for one swallow," then we could say that he was not prospering. But he said, "My cup runneth over." Any time a thing is running over, that is a sign of abundance. If the cup is running over, then that means that there is more than enough.

Think about Luke 6:38: **Give, and it shall be given unto you;** *good measure, pressed down, and shaken together, and running over....* That means abundance! Let me give you a practical illustration to enhance the point I'm making.

I had heard for quite a few years about a trash compactor for the home. Commercial businesses have been using this type of equipment for years, but then the manufacturers began making these appliances for the home too. When they first came out, I said, "We don't need a trash compactor; we've got plenty of trash cans." Then I began to notice that every time I would go to the trash can or basket in the house, it would be full. It was absolutely astounding the amount of trash you can accumulate in the course of a week without realizing it. The big basket on the back porch was always full. I had to take that thing out almost every other day, at least — sometimes every day. It would be empty when I left home in the morning, but by the time I got back in the evening, it would be running over. Finally I came to the point that I got tired of that, so I said, "I'm going to buy a trash compactor."

So I bought one. I got the biggest size available for home use. *I was amazed!* We could go a whole week without having to take out the trash — even more than a week, part way into the next week! I have discovered a secret about compacting trash. I turn the machine on and get it going in the down cycle. When it gets to the bottom of the cycle, it makes a very small pause before it starts back up. Once it gets down to the bottom of the cycle, I hit the stop button and that keeps constant pressure on the trash. Every bit of air that is in there is squeezed out, and I can get even more trash compacted.

That's what the Bible means when it says, ". . .good measure, pressed down, and shaken together, and running over. . . ."

It's not like a little bit of trash down at the bottom of the basket, it's like trash in ". . .good measure, pressed down, and shaken together, and running over." That's abundance! *And the Bible is full of abundance — God's abundant blessings that He wants His children to have!*

Why would any Christian want to *deny* the validity of the prosperity message? Really, anyone who would do that is dishonest, because there is no one who fights or speaks against the message of prosperity who would work this year on the same job doing the same work for less pay that he got last year or the year before. Everyone is always looking for a raise. No union would accept deliberation over a new contract if its leaders came back from the meeting room and announced: "Last year you were making a dollar an hour, but we've settled for 75 cents an hour. Last year you worked a 40-hour week, and we've got a better deal; now you're going to work 48 hours per week. Last year you had three weeks paid vacation, and we've worked out a deal where you will have only a week and a half of vacation."

Nobody would accept a deal like that! People don't want to accept the status quo or less than they had before. As far as pay is concerned, they are always wanting more.

People who oppose the prosperity message say, "Well, this prosperity business can't be from God, because those who preach it talk too much about material things." Yet that is what they are working for. I'll wager that there is not one of them who is working for free. There is not one of them who works for an employer or even in a ministry who says, "I don't want to get paid; I just want to work, I don't need the money."

God Is Our Source

In my own ministry, I get paid a salary for serving as pastor of Crenshaw Christian Center. That's my job. Like a doctor or a lawyer or a ditch digger, I get paid for what I do. We all work and get a salary. That's how we make our living. But the pay that I receive for being a pastor is not my source. I have learned that if Crenshaw Christian Center folded and went out of business (which it's not going to do), I wouldn't lose anything *because God is not out of business!* If God ever goes out of business, we will have a problem — a gigantic, "humongous," giant economy-sized problem.

But for a company to go out of business is a problem for those who work for it — that is, if they don't know how to believe and act on the Word of God. Their job is only one of the many available channels that God can use at any given time to pipe resources to them. If that source dries up, it doesn't mean that God has dried up. It just means that He will have to find another channel to use.

That is how you operate independent of the system. When I say, "the system," I am speaking of the world's "set up" — the economic and financial system of the world, which is designed to keep the average person from getting ahead.

There are certain people who are controlling the economies of the world. A few people who have staggering amounts of wealth control the rest of the world through the system. The system was never designed to help you get ahead. It was designed to keep you chained to your typewriter or to the engine you operate on the assembly line. It was designed to keep you tied to that machine while you produce the goods that the wealthy can enjoy.

Have you ever noticed that getting a raise doesn't do you any good (unless you get an astronomical raise, like moving from $20,000 a year to $40,000 annually)?

Have you ever noticed that every time you get a raise, the cost of living goes up to consume that extra income? Sometimes you end up worse off than you were before your salary increase, because the cost of living goes up faster than your salary. Have you ever noticed that? You really don't get ahead by getting a raise in pay. The only way a raise can help you is if the economy stays the same in terms of the cost of living. *But it doesn't!*

Everything seems to escalate side by side. You get a raise, and right away the price of food, clothing and housing goes up. You can't take your raise and say,

"Okay, I've lived on $20,000 a year, so now that I have got a raise and will be making $25,000, I'll have $5,000 to put into savings." No, it doesn't work that way. Because the price of everything you buy is going to go up along with your raise in pay.

Besides prices, there is the graduated income tax. You make a certain amount of money, fine! If you escalate to a higher level of income, you simply move into a higher tax bracket. You may well end up paying more taxes and having less money to spend than you did before your income increased.

This is not to be pessimistic. What I am trying to do is show you why the world's system operates against the message of prosperity — it wants to keep you locked into the system. While you are locked into the system, you can't give away the $10,000 you would like to give to the work of the Lord because you need every nickel you make just to live on. If the system can keep you struggling, then you won't have anything left over to give away. If Christians don't have anything to give, then the outreaches of ministries are going to be curtailed because the only people who are going to support ministries are Christians. But if the Body of Christ doesn't have anything to give, then ministries will come to a standstill because they won't have the money they need to stay in operation.

The system operates on the basic principle: "We don't loan money to churches." This is a calculated plan to thwart the work of God. *But God has a way to bless us over and above the system!* However, you will have to learn how to operate by faith to get into God's plan.

22

Prosperity *Is* God's Will!

You can be the most dedicated Christian possible and still struggle financially, economically and materially. I did it for 17 years. Yes, I've been there! I know what it's like to be in want and in need. I have a master's degree in struggling. That's the reason I don't back down to anyone concerning God's Word on prosperity. I couldn't care less what people think or what they say about it. *Prosperity* may not be for them, but I guarantee you that if there is only one person on this planet that it is for — *it is me!*

Prosperity may not be for you, but it's definitely for me. My name is all through the Bible. When it says, "The Lord is my shepherd," that means He is Fred's shepherd. When it says, "Thou preparest a table before me," it is talking about *me*, Fred Price. I don't care what anybody thinks about me; people can think what they please, it doesn't bother me in the least. When all my bills are paid, and I have money in my pocket, in the bank and to give away because the Lord has honored my stand on His Word, do you think I care what people may think?

What God will do for one, He will do for all — all those, that is, who take Him at His Word. Romans 2:11 says, **...there is no respect of persons with God.** *I love it!* There are some groups of people in the world who do respect persons, but we don't have to be concerned about them, because they are not our source. *God,* our Father, *is our source!*

Third John 2 states, **Beloved, I wish above all things that thou mayest prosper....** If God is no respector of persons, then He could not want one or two groups of people to prosper and the rest of society to be in lack and want. Because, if He did, He would be a respector of persons, and that would invalidate His Word. God treats everyone the same — that is, everyone who will make the commitment to do things His way. *The qualifier is doing things His way!* You *must* be in tune, as it were, and in harmony and in agreement with God's way in order to receive His best. If you are in agreement with God's way — which is outlined in His Word — then He is no respector of persons, as far as you are concerned. If He blesses one person, then He has obligated Himself to bless you or me or anyone else who will make a stand on His Word of promise.

Prosperity is for the total man: spirit, soul and body!

However, you have to consider each entity separately. As previously stated in this book, I am primarily dealing with the material aspects of prosperity. This is not all I teach, and it certainly is not all I know, but it's a valid part of life that the Christian needs to grasp if he is going to be an effective force for God in this world.

The thing about it that's so bad is that the prosperity message has been an understated part of life and has been talked down, criticized, and even rejected for so long that one almost has to be or appear to be fanatical and go to the extreme to get things into right perspective.

For example, a ship is supposed to ride the water on what is called an "even keel." This means that the ship is supposed to lie flat, geometrically in line with the horizon, sitting level in the water. If the ship should spring a leak, causing it to take in a lot of water, it won't float. There is a law that says that a hollowed-out ship full of water cannot float. If every air space becomes filled with water, that ship is going to sink to the bottom of the sea.

Another thing that will happen is that a ship filling up with water on one side will "list," which means that it will lean toward the side where the water is coming in. A ship can list so badly that it's almost on its side — it may still be floating at this juncture, but over on its side. In order to get that ship righted, you have to go to the opposite side and apply enormous pressure to get it back to an even keel.

That's the way the old ship of Zion has been going — it has listed so far to one side with erroneous doctrine or no doctrine, false teaching and faulty instruction, or mixed-up and messed-up instruction, that you almost have to appear to be completely fanatical to right the old ship and get her back on an even keel!

Some Christians not only need to get back on an even keel, they also need to get level with God's plan of prosperity in the first place — *they've never been there!* They don't even know that they are supposed to be prosperous. They think that whatever happens is God's will.

Whatever happens is not always God's will!

It may be in His *permissive* will, but it certainly is not in His *decreed* will. It is true that everything that happens on this earth, God allows to take place. But to allow something and to decree something are two different things.

25

Everything that happens on this planet God allows to take place. Otherwise it couldn't occur. If it could, then whatever it is that happened would be a stronger force than God. Of course, we know that there is no force stronger than God; consequently, we have to say that God allows, or permits, certain things to take place. But that does not mean that He decrees them to happen.

For example, I am sure that at the very moment you are reading this page some woman somewhere is being raped or even murdered. Someone is committing adultery, stealing, robbing, killing, or what have you. And God is allowing these terrible things to happen. But I am also sure that He is *not* saying, "It is My will for that man to rape that woman, slash her throat and leave her dead in a ditch." No! That is not God's will! It is not God's will that kids shoot up heroine and sniff cocaine and eventually blow their brains out. There is a difference in the decreed will of God and the permissive will of God. He has to permit things to happen because He gave man a free will. If we permit something, God has to permit it. Many people don't understand that principle. They think that because something happens, God approves of it. No, God doesn't have anything to do with much of what takes place on this earth day by day. What happens here is up to us! Let me prove it by the Bible.

> **Verily, I say unto you, Whatsoever *ye* shall bind on earth shall be bound in heaven: and whatsoever *ye* shall loose on earth shall be loosed in heaven.**
> **Matthew 18:18**

Notice what the Lord is saying in this verse. He is *not* saying: "Verily, I say unto you, Whatsoever I shall

bind on earth shall be bound in heaven: and whatsoever I shall loose on earth shall be loosed in heaven."

Notice where the binding and loosing begin.
Where? In earth — not in heaven. The ball is in our
court. God says, "Whatever *you* loose on earth will be
loosed in heaven." This does not mean that if you and
I loose murder on earth, murder will be loosed in
heaven. There is no murder in heaven. What God is
saying in this verse of scripture is, *"Whatever you do down
here I have to ratify in heaven. I have to say yea and amen
to it in heaven, because you have the first move, and whatever
you do is what is going to be done."*

God does not control our destiny, we do!

2

The Blessing of the Lord, It Maketh Rich!

Christ hath redeemed us from the curse of the law, being made a curse for us: for it is written, Cursed is every one that hangeth on a tree:

That the blessing of Abraham might come on the Gentiles through Jesus Christ; that we might receive the promise of the Spirit through faith.

Galatians 3:13,14

Verse 14 of this passage does not mean to say that we are going to receive the Holy Spirit as a gift. When it says, "the promise of the Spirit," it means that it was the Spirit of God Who gave the promise to Abraham.

In other words, God, through His Spirit, made the promise. This is not talking about receiving the Spirit. Not here, it's not. That's what it looks like it may be saying. If you're not careful, you could get that impression.

Here's what I want you to see: In verse 13, we read that "Christ hath redeemed us from the curse of the law. . . ." In verse 14, we are told the reason Christ did this — "That the blessing of Abraham might come on the *Gentiles . . . .*"

If a person is not a Jew, then he is a Gentile. This passage says that Jesus was crucified that the blessing of Abraham might come upon the Gentiles. Therefore, if you and I are Gentiles, then we qualify to receive the blessing of Abraham. All we have to do is find out how Abraham was blessed, then we will know what the blessing of Abraham was which we are to receive.

If Abraham was blessed spiritually, then we know that it is spiritual blessings that are going to come upon us. If he was blessed "soulishly," then we know that it is "soulish" blessings that we are promised. If he was blessed materially, then we know that it is material blessings that we can expect to receive from God.

The Blessing of Abraham: Spiritual or Material?

Now the Lord had said unto Abram, Get thee out of thy country, and from thy kindred, and from thy father's house, unto a land that I will shew thee:

And I will make of thee a great nation, and I will bless thee, and make thy name great; and thou shalt be a blessing.

Genesis 12:1,2

Abraham did not live in the day in which Jesus Christ lived. Therefore, he could not have accepted Jesus as his personal Savior and Lord, which means that Abraham could not have been born again. So if Abraham was not born again, then really from a spiritual standpoint, he was a sinner.

Everybody under the Old Testament was a sinner. They may have been servants of God, and they may have said yes to God's Word — the amount of Word that they had under the Old Covenant — but from a spiritual viewpoint, they were still sinners. They were operating with a dead spiritual nature, dead to God.

Since Abraham was not, and could not have been born again, he could not have received any *spiritual* blessing from God, because he was actually cut off from God. God dealt with Abraham just as He dealt with anyone else under the Old Covenant. He dealt with them all primarily from a physical standpoint. He had to. That's why He gave them the Law. The Law had nothing to do with their spirits. It was all fleshly oriented. It had to do with the physical body.

God dealt with Israel through the flesh. That's all He could do. He couldn't deal with them through the spirit, so He condescended. In other words, man under the Old Covenant could not come up to God's level; therefore, God, out of His tender mercies and loving kindness, came down to man's level and dealt with him in the flesh. Man at that time was not able to come to God and approach Him as we can under the New Covenant.

With that bit of knowledge, we can know a part of what this 14th verse means: "That *the blessing of Abraham* might come on the Gentiles...."

We know right now that the blessing of Abraham could not have been a spiritual blessing. Well, what is left?

There are only two worlds: the spiritual world, and the physical world. There is no third world. No in-between world. Either you and I are in the spiritual realm, or we are in the physical realm.

31

A Great Name

Now let's go back to Genesis 12:2: "And I will make of thee a great nation, and I will bless thee, and *make thy name great....*"

God said that He would bless Abraham and make his name great. Your name can't be great if you yourself are small. If your name is great, you are great. You can't separate a person from his name. You can't say that a person is great, but his name is lousy. So when God said that He would bless Abraham and make of him a great nation and make his name great, the way He was going to make Abraham's name great was by making Abraham great.

Have you ever heard of John D. Rockefeller? Now what does that name say to you? Money? Other than the fact that he was fabulously wealthy, you probably don't know anything about John D. Rockefeller. You don't know if he was tall or short, fat or thin, educated or uneducated. The only thing you can relate to John D. Rockefeller is money, and a whole lot of it. What made him great? His wealth made him great. His name became synonymous with his riches. Otherwise he would be just another John Doe. Of itself, the name Rockefeller is no better than the name Jackson or Johnson. The name is nothing. It is what is behind the name that is important.

So when God said that He was going to bless Abraham and make his name great, He was telling Him: "I'm going to bless you, and I'm going to make *you* great."

"I will make you a blessing..."

Notice the rest of verse 2: "And I will make of thee a great nation, and I will bless thee, and make thy name great: *and thou shalt be a blessing.*"

You can't be a blessing until you are blessed yourself. You have to be blessed in order to become a blessing to others.

"...to all the families of the earth."

And I will bless them that bless thee, and curse him that curseth thee: and in thee shall *all families of the earth be blessed.*

Genesis 12:3

God is saying here, "Abraham, I am going to bless you, and then the people are going to bless you. Then, because of you, I am going to bless the people who bless you, all the families of the whole earth."

This is great!

This verse says the same thing that Paul said in Galatians about being blessed, but it still doesn't tell us from a definite standpoint exactly what the blessings were. So, let's move on to something else.

Abraham Was Very Rich!

And Abram went up out of Egypt, he, and his wife, and all that he had, and Lot with him, into the south.

And Abram was very rich in cattle, in silver, and in gold.

Genesis 13:1,2

Here the Holy Ghost categorically tells us how Abraham was blessed. No one can mess up this statement with his "Mickey Mouse," five-cents' worth of gray matter, and his two-day education. No one can say, "Well, the blessing of God is spiritual, Brother Price."

In verse 2 of this passage, we are clearly told: "...Abram was very *rich* in cattle, in silver, and in gold."

Cattle. Silver. Gold. You can't mess that up. Thank God, the bishop, the evangelist, the Sunday school teacher, the black folks, the white folks, the Jew, the Gentile, or anybody else — *nobody* — can mess this up. We have it documented in *the Book.*

Thank God for all that I gained from school, but one thing that I am so glad about is that I learned how to read. Nobody can cheat me out of this, because I can read!

Notice what this verse does *not* say. *It does not say that Abraham was rich;* the Bible records that he was *very* rich! It doesn't say that he was almost rich. It doesn't say that he was a little rich. It says that the man was *very* rich. Then it tells us how he was rich: in cattle, in silver, and in gold!

Now tell me if cattle and silver and gold are spiritual. How readest thou?

Think about it. Abraham wasn't even a Christian. He wasn't even saved or born again. He wasn't filled with the Spirit. He didn't have a covenant as good as ours, and yet the man was *very* rich!

Notice in the 12th chapter, God said that He was going to bless Abraham. From that I think we can safely conclude that in the 13th chapter it was God Who had made Abraham rich. But for more proof, we will read from the 24th chapter of Genesis — and then get ready to put on your dancing shoes!

God Blessed Abraham with Riches

In the 24th chapter of Genesis, we have the story in which Abraham sent one of his servants to find a wife for his son Isaac. This was the custom at that time. I don't know what nationality the servant was, whether he was a Hebrew or not; but at any rate, he apparently had picked up on what he had seen his master Abraham do, because he prayed and asked God for guidance in fulfilling his task. Smart man!

He went to a certain place where he actually ended up with some of the relatives of Abraham and his wife Sarah. He came to a certain city, and as the women of that area came to the well to draw water, he asked the Lord to direct him to the one He had chosen to be a wife for his master's son. He ended up in the house of a man named Laban, and here is the rest of the story:

> And Rebekah had a brother, and his name was Laban: and Laban ran out unto the man, unto the well.
>
> And it came to pass, when he saw the earring and bracelets upon his sister's hands, and when he heard the words of Rebekah his sister, saying, Thus spake the man unto me; that he came unto the man; and, behold, he stood by the camels at the well.
>
> And he said, Come in, thou blessed of the Lord; wherefore standest thou without? for I have prepared the house, and room for the camels.
>
> And the man came into the house: and he ungirded his camels, and gave straw and provender for the camels, and water to wash his feet, and the men's feet that were with him.

And there was set meat before him to eat: but he said, I will not eat, until I have told mine errand. And he said, Speak on.

And he said, I am Abraham's servant.

And the Lord hath blessed my master greatly; and he is become great: and he hath given him flocks, and herds (this is the cattle we read about), and silver (this is the silver), and gold (here is the gold), and menservants, and maidservants, and camels, and asses.

And Sarah my master's wife bare a son to my master when she was old: and unto him hath he given all that he hath.

Genesis 24:29-36

Here it is spelled out very clearly in verse 35: "And *the Lord hath blessed him greatly;* and he is become great: and *he hath given him. . . ."*

Let's paraphrase that verse: "And the Lord has blessed my master greatly." Or we could say it this way: "And the Lord has blessed Abraham greatly, and Abraham has become great. And the Lord has given Abraham flocks, and herds, and silver, and gold, and menservants, and maidservants, and camels, and asses."

Oh, that's out of sight! You have to be deaf, dumb, blind or dishonest not to see that this is talking about material blessings.

Notice that the word "blessed" is used in this verse. We read it in Galatians 3:13,14 which spoke of "the blessing of Abraham." How did God bless Abraham? With *cattle, gold, menservants, maidservants, camels, and asses* (donkeys, burros, or whatever).

36

Abraham was blessed materially.

Blessing Versus Cursing

The Bible says that Christ gave His life that the blessing of Abraham might come on the Gentiles. Well, I am in Christ, and I am a Gentile, so there is no doubt about who is supposed to be blessed: *me! — and any other believer who is willing to believe, receive and act on the Word of God!*

Galatians 3:13 says that Christ has redeemed us from the curse of the Law, that the blessing of Abraham might come upon us. We want to find out what that curse and that blessing is.

What Is the Curse of the Law?

When I am teaching, I am always happy when I get to Deuteronomy 28 because I know that faith comes by hearing and hearing and hearing. (Rom. 10:17.) Some folks get tired of hearing the Word. I don't ever get tired of hearing it. Every time I hear it, I get more faith.

In the 28th chapter of Deuteronomy, we find a description of the blessings of the Law, and the curse of the Law. In other words, what will come upon us for being either obedient or disobedient to the Word of God. The Law is ultimately God's Word. Don't just get locked into the Ten Commandments or the first five books of the Bible, which are usually referred to from a historical standpoint as "the Law."

Anything God tells us to do or not to do is law.

God never makes suggestions. When the Lord tells us to do something, that is not a suggestion. He doesn't mean that we are to do it if we can work it into our schedule. When He tells us to do something, He means for us to do it. Not just think about it, but *do it!* God's Law is God's Word — God's Word is God's Law.

In the 28th chapter of Deuteronomy, it is interesting to note that there are 68 verses. Only 14 describe the blessing and 54 describe the curse. I believe the reason for this is because God wants us to understand the enormity of the curse so that we will avoid it as we would avoid the Bubonic plague.

Take time to read all 68 verses of this passage. You will find them interesting. Especially note the curse part. I am going to cover the blessing part, but you most definitely need to be aware of the curse part as well. If you don't know what you've been redeemed from, sometimes you don't have as much appreciation for what you've been redeemed to.

At the time the Law was given to the children of Israel, the original recipients of the blessings and cursings of Deuteronomy 28, they were basically an agricultural society, being mainly farmers, husbandmen — herders of sheep, cattle and goats. Quite naturally, the blessings and cursings centered around their mainstream of life, their primary livelihood. However, the same principles enumerated in this chapter still apply to us today regardless of our occupation or station in life.

God's Word endures forever!

The Blessings of Obedience

And it shall come to pass, if thou shalt hearken diligently unto the voice of the Lord thy God, to

observe and to do all his commandments which I command thee this day, that the Lord thy God will set thee on high above all nations of the earth:

And all these blessings shall come on thee, and overtake thee, if thou shalt hearken unto the voice of the Lord thy God.

Blessed shalt thou be in the city, and blessed shalt thou be in the field.

Blessed shall be the fruit of thy body, and the fruit of thy ground, and the fruit of thy cattle, the increase of thy kine, and the flocks of thy sheep.

Blessed shall be thy basket and thy store.

Blessed shalt thou be when thou comest in, and blessed shalt thou be when thou goest out.

The Lord shall cause thine enemies that rise up against thee to be smitten before thy face: they shall come out against thee one way, and flee from before thee seven ways.

The Lord shall command the blessing upon thee in thy storehouses, and in all that thou settest thine hand unto; and he shall bless thee in the land which the Lord thy God giveth thee.

The Lord shall establish thee an holy people unto himself, as he hath sworn unto thee, if thou shalt keep the commandments of the Lord thy God, and walk in his ways.

And all people of the earth shall see that thou art called by the name of the Lord; and they shall be afraid of thee.

And the Lord shall make thee plenteous in goods, in the fruit of thy body, and in the fruit of thy cattle, and in the fruit of thy ground, in the land which the Lord sware unto thy fathers to give thee.

The Lord shall open unto thee his good treasure, the heaven to give the rain unto thy land in his season, and to bless all the work of thine hand: and thou shalt lend unto many nations, and thou shalt not borrow.

And the Lord shall make thee the head, and not the tail; and thou shalt be above only, and thou shalt not be beneath; if that thou hearken unto the commandments of the Lord thy God, which I command thee this day, to observe and to do them:

And thou shalt not go aside from any of the words which I command thee this day, to the right hand, or to the left, to go after other gods to serve them.

Deuteronomy 28:1-14

Praise God for these great promises and blessings. *They belong to us* — and we, as the Body of Christ, have a right to claim them, possess them, and make them a part of our daily confessions!

3

Trust God, Not Uncertain Riches

When I first got saved, there was some emphasis placed on the idea that Christians were not supposed to have material wealth. As believers we could survive and have enough to get along on, but we were never to seek after material wealth. We were supposed to look forward to the day when we would have ours "over on the other side" — in the "sweet bye and bye."

It is a fact of life that there are many things in this world that are good, nice, lovely, exquisite and desirable. But according to some people, Christians are not to be involved in the pursuit or acquisition of the material goods of this life because these things are classified as "worldly."

However, until we begin to walk in the spirit and walk by faith, we will never really understand that Christians have a right to (and should be the ones to enjoy) the good things of life because of Jesus and the awesome price He paid to bring us salvation and all that it entails. And the only reason people do not understand this truth is because they have been deceived.

There has been a rigorous effort on the part of the devil and his demonic forces to infiltrate the Christian community with false teaching. When I use this term "Christian community," I am talking about all Christians collectively, whether they be in a local church setting or in their individual home setting.

Periodically, I will receive a letter from someone, or I will run into someone, who is very down on Christians having material wealth. Such people feel that a person is not very spiritual if he possesses an abundance of this world's goods. However, the Bible does not support this idea, because in order to get the job done that Jesus started, *it is going to take material possessions — namely wealth!*

To make such a statement in the Christian world is a "no-no." Many believers use the "cop out" that if you look at things that way, you might be tempted to make the pursuit of money your primary aim in life.

Well, you might be tempted to do that even if you don't look at wealth in that way!

Folks have been known to make money their prime goal in life wihout being Christian at all. For any and every thing you do, there is a risk factor involved — a risk that you might go to the extreme, the risk that you might go wrong. But you can do that anyway. Consequently, to me this excuse is not a legitimate reason for shying away or steering away from some of the things that some people say Christians ought not to be involved in.

This is a deception of Satan to hinder the work of God. Everything about the Gospel costs money. It is really only when you are working in full-time ministry that you understand what is involved in spreading the Gospel. Then you can really see why the devil fights so tenaciously to keep us ignorant of our covenant rights and ignorant of the fact that God does want us to have material things. God has never been opposed to Christians having things — God is opposed to material things having Christians, and there is as much difference between these two as night and day.

"Charge them that are rich..."

Charge them that are rich in this world, that they be not highminded, nor trust in uncertain riches, but in the living God, who giveth us richly all things to enjoy.

1 Timothy 6:17

"Charge them that are rich *in this world....*" Here we know that Paul is talking about this earth — this planet — *not heaven* — because he says, "in this world." This is to distinguish between the spirit world and the three-dimensional physical world. If he had said, "Charge them that are *rich in the spirit*," or "*rich in God*," or "*rich in the things of God*," then we could say that earthly riches are not for the Christian.

"...that they be not highminded..."

In other words, don't allow the fact that you are rich to influence your mind to the point where you begin to think that you are better than anyone else, or that because you are rich you can get away with anything you like.

Many times this is what happens to a lot of "rich" people. They get to the point where they really think they are above the law. They get to thinking, "Hey, you can't touch me, I am So and So!" They throw their weight around — their "wealth weight," so to speak.

Yes, a wealthy person can become highminded. But I know some highminded folks who don't have a pot to cook in. A person can be highminded whether he possesses any of this world's goods or not.

So that is the first point Paul is making here: "Be not highminded." But notice what else he has to say in this verse.

> **"...nor trust in uncertain riches, but in the living God...."**

The reason the Bible says "uncertain riches" is because riches change. Values change, and riches are only as good as the present value system. What is valuable today might not be worth anything tomorrow. Or what is worthless today may be extremely valuable tomorrow. The value of currency changes. Therefore, if all a person trusts is riches, and then a radical change in the value system occurs, he is in trouble because his trust is in his material wealth.

Notice the word "rich." This word is interesting; it literally means *"abundantly* (copiously or lavishly) *supplied."* This is what the inference is in this verse. Obviously this has to do with us becoming channels to bless other people.

You and I don't need an abundance to meet our own needs; we only need *enough.*

For instance, if I have a loan of $5,000 to pay off in monthly installments of $25, all I need each month is $25; I don't need $26. I could use $5,000 to pay off the whole debt, but really all I need in terms of my monthly obligation is $25. As long as I have that amount each month I am safe and free; everything is taken care of.

So if I come to the end of the pay period with $250 left over and I only need $25 of it to pay my monthly bill, then I am abundantly supplied. I then have the option, or the opportunity, to squander the extra cash on myself, or use it to be a channel of blessing to someone else.

But you and I can never get to be a blessing to others until we are abundantly, copiously, lavishly supplied ourselves so that all our own needs are taken care of. Then we can become a channel of blessing to others.

There Is Plenty for All!

The way God blesses people is through other people. God does not drop money down out of the sky. It comes through the hands of people. Some way, some how it comes through the system, because everything that we need is already available in the system. God has stocked this world with all that is needed.

Every once in a while, people start talking about running out of some vital resource; we are not going to run out of anything. To run out of something is to say that God has been caught short, that He did not know how long His children would have to be here before Jesus came back, and that He has let us come up short of what we need to get by on until Jesus returns. God is never caught short.

All shortages that we hear about are man-made; they are created to drive prices up or down or whatever. It is all designed for a few folks to make more money. There is no shortage of anything. Nothing is short.

Everything is systematically designed to keep the average person grovelling in the dust.

When you keep a person struggling to get his needs met, you keep him under control. When he becomes independently wealthy, he is difficult to control. But as long as he is dependent upon the system, then it is as though he is handcuffed to his job or machine or whatever it is that contributes to his sustenance.

Economics is a systematic way of making the rich richer and of keeping the average person producing for the wealthy. Economics is a contrived system. Things don't just happen, they are made to happen. There is no shortage of anything that man needs to survive, but shortages are deliberately created to make more money for those in control. Everything is about making money. It is greed and the love of mammon that keep the world's economic system going, that keeps the wheels turning.

Friend, if the work force did not show up for work for 30 days, this nation would come to a screeching halt — we would be in big trouble. If the average person did not do his job on a daily basis, this whole system would come to a standstill. Can you imagine what would happen if the farmer stopped farming? Can you imagine what would be the result if the dairyman stopped milking? We would have some real serious problems.

There is plenty of everything!

What we have to learn to do as Christians is to cut into the pie and get our piece. But not just for us, but so we can be a channel that God can use to marshal the resources under the control of the Body of Christ to get the message and the Gospel to the masses. In the process of doing that, all our needs will be taken care of. But if all we have time to do is spend our every waking moment making ends meet, we will never get to the point where we will have anything left over for someone else.

Riches Are Not Evil

First Timothy 6:17 tells me that there is nothing wrong with riches. If there were something intrinsically wrong with riches, the Lord through the Apostle Paul would have said, "Charge them that are rich in this world *to get rid of their wealth.*" If God knew that you had hold of something that was dangerous, something that could be harmful or hurtful to you, then as a wise Father He would do everything in His power to see to it that you were separated from that thing. Yet He did not say to those who are rich, "Get rid of your wealth," but rather He said two things to them: 1) "don't be highminded," and 2) "don't trust in riches."

I want to thoroughly cover this area because this Bible principle needs to get into peoples' spirits so that it can begin to affect their souls or their minds in order to direct their bodies.

Think about this: consider the average person who devotes every day of his life to rising from bed, getting dressed, driving to work, spending a minimum of eight hours on the job, then coming back home to complete the employment cycle. The average person uses up most of his waking moments in making a living.

If you are an average working man or woman, you are not getting rich, you are not getting ahead, you are just surviving. Like most people, you are in a survival mode, and that takes up the majority of your waking hours. Think about what could happen if you did not have to use all that time trying to provide for your own needs. Think what it would be like if you could use that time to become independent of the circumstances of life so you could amass wealth for the purpose of making yourself totally available to God as a channel of blessing, instead of expending all of your time and energy trying to make it to another step or plateau financially.

With regard to this area of trusting not in uncertain riches, let's look at an incident in the life of Jesus which we find recorded in the Gospel of Mark.

The Case of the Rich Young Ruler

And when he was gone forth into the way, there came one running, and kneeled to him, and asked him, Good Master, what shall I do that I may inherit eternal life?

Mark 10:17

"And when he was gone forth...., *there came one running,* and kneeled to him...." Notice that Jesus was not the one who was running; the one running came and kneeled before Him and called Him "Good Master."

Let's see what this young man wanted from Jesus. "....what shall I do that I may inherit eternal life?" This man was aware that he did not have eternal life, and he wanted to find out about it. So He came running to the Master, asking Him about this vital subject which concerned him so much.

> And Jesus said unto him, Why callest thou me good? there is none good but one, that is, God.
>
> Thou knowest the commandments, Do not commit adultery, Do not kill, Do not steal, Do not bear false witness, Defraud not, Honour thy father and mother.
>
> **Mark 10:18,19**

Every person brought up as an Israelite knew the commandments by heart. Whether he obeyed them or not, each individual Jew knew God's laws from childhood. It was standard procedure in Hebrew homes for the parents to teach their children the Law, so that almost without exception every Israelite knew what God required of His people.

> And he answered and said unto him, Master, all these have I observed from my youth.
>
> **Mark 10:20**

This is marvelous. This young man did not say that he had observed some of these commandments, or that he had observed a few of them since high school or early adulthood — the man said that he had observed *all* of these commandments *from his youth.*

Can you imagine any person today being able to say that he has never borne false witness (never lied), never committed adultery (never had sex outside of marriage), never killed, never stolen or defrauded, never failed to honor his father and mother?

That's why so many people today can't imagine being prosperous — because they know they have not been living right before God!

"...*all* these have I observed...." This is absolutely astounding. And this man was not even saved, he was

49

not even filled with the Holy Spirit, he did not even have a covenant as good as the Christian's. Yet he could say: "...all these have I observed from my youth."

> **Then Jesus beholding him loved him, and said unto him, One thing thou lackest: go thy way, sell whatsoever thou hast, and give to the poor, and thou shalt have treasure in heaven: and come, take up the cross, and follow me.**
>
> **And he was sad at that saying, and went away grieved: for he had great possessions.**
>
> **Mark 10:21,22**

A moment ago, this man had come running. He did not walk at a brisk pace, he came running and kneeling. Now he is sad at what he hears, and goes away grieving. Why? "...because he had great possessions."

I want to use this verse to illustrate a point which many Christians hardly seem to realize. *Where did this young man get his "great possessions"? He got them from God!* And he was not even a Christian. The reason he got them from God was because he followed the Law!

The Bible says that God does not change, that there is not even a shadow of changing with God. (Mal. 3:6; James 1:17.) If God desires poverty for His children today, then He had to be in favor of poverty for His family back then. But this man had great possessions — that is not poverty — and he got them by keeping the Law.

I am well persuaded (and I plan definitely to ask the Lord about this when I see Him) that verse 22 of this passage is incorrectly interpreted. (Notice that I said "I believe" — me, Fred Price.) I'm not speaking for anyone else, but I sincerely believe that this verse should read like this: "And he was sad at that saying, and went away grieved: *for great possessions had him.*"

It is obvious that this was the case, because his possessions had such a tight grip on him that he could not turn loose of them. You talk about having a monkey on your back. This young man had a monkey on his back, his chest, his head, and standing on his toes. *He could not give up his possessions, even for eternal life.*

It was obvious that the possessions had him. That is the danger with things. If people are not careful, they can allow things to control them. That is the danger of possessions. But that is the same as saying that there is a great danger of driving on a mountain road in the middle of a storm, because you might get too close to the edge and go over. You don't have to go over! Drive close to the mountain, and you will not go over the edge.

It is just that simple. We don't need to be intimidated by the devil and cheated or robbed of what God wants us to have by listening to the lies of Satan who tells us: "Well, you know, if you get all that stuff, it is going to control you. It is going to own you. It is going to dictate to you."

No! No! No! It cannot, unless you let it!

". . .go. . .sell whatsoever thou hast, and give to the poor. . . ."

I want to show you something else that people have missed — I missed it myself for years:

"Then Jesus beholding him loved him, and said unto him, One thing thou lackest: *go thy way, sell*

whatsoever thou hast, and give to the poor, and thou shalt
have treasure in heaven: and come, take up the cross,
and follow me."

Most people, when they read this verse, interpret
it to mean that Jesus was saying to the man that he was
to go and sell everything that he possessed and give
all the proceeds from the sale to the poor— meaning
that the man would be left with nothing.

That is not what this verse is saying at all!

All Jesus said to the man was for him to sell what
he had and give to the poor. He did not say, "Sell what
you have and give to the poor *everything you get from
the sale of what you own."* That would have left the man
with nothing.

The man came to Jesus and said that he wanted
eternal life. How was he going to get eternal life? In order
to get it, he would have to physically follow Jesus,
because at that time there were no local churches as
we have them today. There were no local pastors as we
know them now. So in order for this man to obtain
eternal life, he would have to follow the *Life Giver.* To
do that, he would have to have an itinerant ministry,
traveling from place to place. It would be a little difficult
to drag along all of his possessions with him.

Jesus wanted this man to turn all of his solid assets
into liquid assets so he could carry them with him. He
said to the man, "Sell everything you own, and give
to the poor." He did not say, "Sell everything you own,
and then give to the poor *everything you get from the sale
of what you have."*

I used to interpret this verse that way, and that is the way most people interpret it. They think that what Jesus was saying was that the man was to be left with nothing. But that would not have brought honor to God. In fact, that would have been a denial of God's provision. Because the reason that the man had great possessions in the first place was because he had followed the Law of God.

Think about it: the man had great possessions, and he had never defrauded anybody, he had never stolen or even cheated on his income taxes — that is most amazing!

Do Not Trust in Riches!

And Jesus looked round about, and saith unto his disciples, How hardly shall they that have riches enter into the kingdom of God!

And the disciples were astonished at his words. But Jesus answereth again, and saith unto them, Children, how hard is it for them that trust in riches to enter into the kingdom of God!

Mark 10:23,24

Doesn't that sound just like 1 Timothy 6:17: "Charge them that are rich in this world, that they be not highminded, *nor trust in uncertain riches,* but in the living God...."?

Now notice what Jesus said in the latter part of verses 23 and 24: "...How hardly shall they that have riches enter into the kingdom of God"; "...how hard is it *for them that trust in riches* to enter the kingdom of God." That is the problem: *trusting in riches* — not the riches themselves.

53

> **It is easier for a camel to go through the eye of a needle, than for a rich man to enter into the kingdom of God.**
>
> Mark 10:25

Notice that Jesus did not say that a rich man could not enter the kingdom, any more than He said that a camel could not go through the eye of a needle. He said it is *easier* for the camel to go through the eye of a needle than for a rich man to enter the kingdom.

> **And they were astonished out of measure, saying among themselves, Who then can be saved?**
>
> **And Jesus looking upon them saith, With men it is impossible, but not with God: for with God all things are possible.**
>
> Mark 10:26,27

If all things are possible, then the rich man can get saved, and a camel can go through the eye of a needle. All God has to do is make a very big needle. We limit God by thinking of a sewing needle; there is no law that says that a needle must be only so large.

> **"...Lo, we have left all...."**
>
> **Then Peter began to say unto him, Lo, we have left all, and have followed thee.**
>
> Mark 10:28

The common concensus today concerning the disciples of Jesus is that they did not have anything, materially speaking. If you do not have anything, you cannot leave anything. If Peter and the other disciples had had nothing but a welfare check coming in, then how could they have said, "...we have left *all*, and have followed thee"?

The Bible does not indicate that the apostles were without material means; in fact, according to Mark's Gospel, Chapter 1, verses 19 and 20, the contrary is indicated:

> **And when he had gone a little further thence, he saw James the son of Zebedee, and John his brother, who also were in the ship mending their nets.**
>
> **And straightway he called them: and they left their father Zebedee in the ship with the hired servants, and went after him.**

"...and they left their father...*with the hired servants....*" If a person has hired servants, he is in good financial shape. This does not sound like somebody who is on welfare.

When Peter said, "We have left all," he was talking about having given up something. The brothers, James and John, were in a fishing business with their father who had hired servants. This indicates that he and his sons were in a pretty good financial condition.

The point I am making is that, in our minds, because of traditional church teaching, we have had the idea that the apostles were just a bunch of itinerant bums, jack-leg preachers, who did not have a pot to cook in and who were running around the countryside barely making it.

Matthew was sitting at the receipt of custom when he was called to follow Jesus. (Matt. 9:9.) If anybody had any money, it was the tax collector, especially in those days when there were no governing bodies to keep control. A collector could tell a person that he owed a thousand dollars in taxes, and then the collector might keep nine hundred for himself and give Caesar a hundred, which Caesar was glad to get. Consequently, the tax people were quite well off.

When Matthew left his job, I do not believe he did so thinking that he was going to leave everything he had without receiving something in return, something better than (or at at least comparable to) what he already had. When Peter said, "We have left *all*," that statement is powerful in its implications, and we have not really seen it in its proper light. Let's go back to Mark 10:29.

A Hundredfold Return

And Jesus answered and said, Verily I say unto you, There is no man that hath left house, or brethren, or sisters, or father, or mother, or wife, or children, or lands, for my sake, and the gospel's,

But he shall receive an hundredfold now in this time (in this life, in this dispensation) houses (not house, but *houses*), and brethren, and sisters, and mothers, and children, and lands, with persecutions: and in the world to come eternal life.

Mark 10:29,30

Jesus is saying here that God wants us to have both: the eternal life, and the houses and lands — "in this time." But we have to put it together in its proper perspective. We also need to add to Mark 10:30 what Jesus said in Matthew 6:33: "But seek ye first the kingdom of God, and his righteousness; and *all these things shall be added unto you.*"

Where some people miss it is that they go out and try to get the things first with the intention of coming back to give God His portion.

You cannot do that!

56

Notice again the latter part of Mark 10:29: ". . .Verily, I say unto you, There is no man that *hath left* house, or brethren, or sisters, or father, or mother, or wife, or children, or lands, for my sake, and the gospel's."

"*. . .hath* left. . . ." There are two ways to leave things: you walk out of your house, and you have left your house; or you give your house away, and you have left your house. You can also walk off and leave your money by becoming separated from it; or you can give your money away, and still become separated from it.

When you give something away for Jesus' sake and the Gospel's, He said that you will receive in return a hundredfold. Don't get caught up in the fact of receiving, but seek first the kingdom, then think about receiving.

You don't get the hundredfold return until you have given something up for the sake of Jesus and the Gospel!

The Value of Tithes and Offerings

The primary thing that we have to give up in our society today is our money. That is why tithes and offerings are so important.

Back in the time in which Jesus lived, people would bring their crops, a sheep or a goat or a lamb, because that was their money. Their wealth was in the possessions that they had. Our society is structured in a different way: our wealth is basically talked about in terms of money. Your net worth is determined by what it comes out to in dollars and cents. You may have lands, you may own a house, a car or even a yacht, but how did you get those things? Basically you had to pay money for them.

In our society, money is the common denominator. Therefore, the thing that we leave for Jesus' sake and the Gospel's is *primarily money.*

Can't you see then the value of tithes and offerings?

Seek the Kingdom, Not Prosperity

You don't get into this Bible principle to get the hundredfold return. Some people shy away from teaching on this subject because they say that they don't want to be a catalyst for folks getting greedy. That is their problem if they get greedy. The truth is still the truth, whether people misunderstand and misuse it or not.

I personally am not going to back off preaching the word of prosperity just because somebody may go out and get greedy. What happens is, they're not going to get greedy — they already are greedy. This principle will simply show up their greed. A person is not greedy because he owns a multitude of things; that is not what makes one greedy! *Greed is a quality some people have whether they own anything of value or not.* Simply accumulating a multitude of possessions is not going to make a person greedy.

Everyone is not going to get greedy, nor make the acquisition of things the end in life. Those who do that are going to do it whether I preach the word of prosperity or whether someone else does. When I preach, I am speaking to the Christians who do not know that prosperity is for them, those who really do not understand prosperity and who are struggling as I was struggling, who are barely surviving as I was barely surviving, those who have been led to believe that Christians are not supposed to have anything in this world.

All of the stories that we read in the Bible have been there all the time. God did not just put the 10th chapter of Mark in the Bible today or yesterday. It has been there since the beginning. That is what is so sad about this whole thing. This chapter was there when my creditors were jacking up my car and repossessing it — and I didn't even know it, because the churches I went to did not tell me. They really didn't even encourage their people to read the Bible. In Hosea 4:6 God said that His people are destroyed for lack of knowledge.

God wants us to be prosperous. He does not want us to seek prosperity for prosperity's sake, but He does want us to enjoy the abundant life that Jesus came to bring us. Prosperity ought to be the result of, and not the thing itself.

Prosperity ought to be the result of a quality of life, commitment and dedication that is in line with God's Word.

Consider again the man who came running to Jesus seeking eternal life. How did he get his possessions? He got those possessions by following the Word of God. With the limited knowledge that he had, he walked in that light, and he had great possessions.

How in the world could God want you and me (who are blood-bought and blood-washed) to struggle and barely make it through life? Here was a man who was not even born again. He came to Jesus asking for eternal life. Jesus did not go to the man and say to him, "I want to give you eternal life." *The man came to Jesus asking what he had to do to inherit salvation* (that's what he was asking about). In essence, what Jesus told him was, *"I am the eternal life now; and in order to get where I am, you have to get beyond what is possessing you."*

That is why Jesus told the man to go and sell what he had. I am well persuaded that if the man had been instantly willing to sell all he owned, Jesus would have said, "Keep it." Because the man had obtained things rightfully; therefore, why should he be deprived of them? He had earned what he had by virtue of the fact that he had kept God's Word, and God had honored His Word in his life.

But Jesus perceived that his possessions were a spiritual obstacle to the man, and the only way that he was going to get the eternal life that Jesus had come to give mankind was by turning loose of that which was keeping him in bondage.

4

The Origin and Purpose of Riches

Charge them that are rich in this world, that they be not highminded, nor trust in uncertain riches, but in the living God, who giveth us richly all things to enjoy.

1 Timothy 6:17

I want to give you another confirming witness concerning riches. There is really no problem with riches, but with the attitude toward them, because riches are neutral. Whether they are good or evil depends on our motive and attitude in terms of the acquisition of material things.

In making my point, I want to use something that is unquestionable, in the sense that nobody can legitimately argue with it — not even the proponents of the idea that Christians are not supposed to have much of what is commonly called "this world's goods." Because of this idea, *the Church* — the Body of Christ — has been limited in its ability to promote the Gospel on the scale that God intends for it to be promoted.

If you have any doubt about God's will for Christians to have material possessions — if you sincerely believe that it is intrinsically wrong for believers to seek after material wealth and earthly possessions — then I would like to point out that in that case it would be equally wrong for Jesus, the Holy Spirit, and God the Father to have material things. In order to be consistent in this teaching, we must admit that it could not be right for God to have material things and His children to have nothing materially.

The Bible says that we are the sons (and, of course, the daughters) of God. Why would God, as a loving Father, want us, His beloved children, to have less than what He has? All things being equal, even earthly fathers want their children to fare better than they themselves. Are we to expect less of our heavenly Father than we do of our earthly fathers?

Let's see what the Word of God has to say regarding riches. First of all, let's go all the way back to the beginning of this planet earth, as we know it, as recorded in the pages of the Bible. We will see that all of the material things that are considered to be valuable, which make for wealth, come out of this earth — *all of them!* Diamonds, emeralds, silver, gold, all the precious metals and their derivatives come out of the earth.

Who created the earth? God did!

If God created the earth, then gold and silver and precious metals could not have come about apart from God. God had to be the Creator of the riches of this earth, if He created the earth itself.

God and His Creation Are Good!

In the beginning God created the heaven and the earth.

And the earth was without form, and void; and darkness was upon the face of the deep. And the Spirit of God moved upon the face of the waters.

62

And God said, Let there be light: and there was light.

And God saw the light, that *it was good;* and God divided the light from the darkness.

And God called the light Day, and the darkness he called Night. And the evening and the morning were the first day.

And God said, Let there be a firmament in the midst of the waters, and let it divide the waters from the waters.

Genesis 1:1-6

If God created the earth, or brought the earth into being, then everything in the earth must be good, because God said that it was good. He did not create it bad. He created it and said that it was good.

It was good because God said that it was good!

That is not to say that it would *stay good*, but as it came from the hand of the Creator, *it was good!* Consequently, everything in the earth, and on it, must be good.

The book of James tells us: **Every good gift and every perfect gift is from above, and cometh down from the Father of lights, with whom is no variableness, neither shadow of turning** (James 1:17). If every good gift comes down from God, then nothing bad can come from God. If there is anything bad, it did not come from God, because the Bible says that "*every* good" comes from Him.

God created two basic kinds of things: one kind had no will of its own, the other had a will. God gave the thing that had a will the greatest and most precious gift in the universe, and that is the gift of *free* will!

Unfortunately, it is in the exercising of this gift that corruption of what is perfect came about.

What is the opposite of light? *Dark.* What is the opposite of up? *Down.* What is the opposite of north? *South.* What is the opposite of male? *Female.* What is the opposite of sin? *Righteousness.* What is the opposite of good? *Bad* or *evil.* Evil is really nothing but a perversion of good! Evil is not something that exists by itself apart from anything else; it is simply the opposite of good. It is when good ceases to be good that it becomes evil. When evil ceases to be evil, it becomes good. Evil has to be a perversion of good; otherwise, God created evil.

There is a verse in the Old Testament which talks about God creating the light and the dark, and the good and the evil. (Is. 45:7.) But if you will study out that passage in the Hebrew, you will find that in the original language this verse was not written that way. The implication is not that God *created* evil, but rather that He *permitted* it.

In the Hebrew there are two senses: *causative* and *permissive.* We only have one sense in English. What happened is that the translators (and why they did this I don't know, since I am not a translator and was not there when this happened), contrary to the Hebrew, placed the verb in the causative sense instead of the permissive sense, which makes it appear that God caused the evil rather than permitting it.

We do have to understand that these translators were not always men ordained of God to do the job. Translations were done by men who saw a need for the Word to be placed into the various languages of the people, and it was because of their scholastic ability that they were given the opportunity to translate the Bible from the original Hebrew and Greek into modern languages. Many translations were made, and while we are grateful for the dedication and work that was done by these early translators, the fact remains that they were not always men anointed of God. That is why we find the foul-ups. God is not fouled up. When He translates through men He has specially anointed to do the job, you are not going to find all these mixed-up words. Had the translators been men called of God, the translations would have been just as God meant them to be, because the Bible says that He is not the author of confusion.

God did not, and does not, create evil.

God cannot be the creator of evil, because there is none in Him. That is why He cannot be responsible for sickness and disease. You cannot give what you don't have. You can only communicate AIDS to another person if you have it yourself. If you don't have it, you cannot pass it on to someone else; you have to have it in some way, form or fashion in order to communicate it. God does not have sickness in Him, so how can He transmit it to you? Sickness is the opposite of health. Sickness is a perversion of good health, just as evil is a perversion of good.

In the book of James, Chapter 1, verse 17, it says, "Every good gift and every perfect gift is from above, and cometh down from the Father of lights, with whom is no variableness, neither shadow of turning." Since every *good* and *perfect* gift comes down from God, sickness, evil and darkness cannot come from above, because there is nothing *good* or *perfect* about them.

> And God said, Let the waters under the heaven be gathered together unto one place, and let the dry land appear: and it was so.
>
> And God called the dry land Earth; and the gathering together of the waters called he Seas: and God saw that it was good.
>
> And God said, Let the earth bring forth grass, the herb yielding seed, and the fruit tree yielding fruit after his kind, whose seed is in itself, upon the earth: and it was so.
>
> And the earth brought forth grass....
>
> **Genesis 1:9-12**

Notice that the Bible does not say that God created grass. It says that God created the earth, and the earth brought forth grass. The grass did not come from God, as such; it came from the earth which God created.

Everything After Its Own Kind

> And the evening and the morning were the third day.
>
> And God said, Let there be lights in the firmament of the heaven to divide the day from the night; and let them be for signs, and for seasons, and for days and years:
>
> And let them be for lights in the firmament of the heaven to give light upon the earth: and it was so.
>
> And God made two great lights; the greater light to rule the day, and the lesser light to rule the night: he made the stars also.

And God set them in the firmament of the heaven to give light upon the earth.

And to rule over the day and over the night, and to divide the light from the darkness: and God saw that it was good.

And the evening and the morning were the fourth day.

And God said, Let the waters bring forth abundantly the moving creature that hath life, and fowl that it may fly above the earth in the open firmament of heaven.

And God created great whales, and every living creature that moveth, which the waters brought forth abundantly, after their kind, and every winged fowl after his kind: and God saw that it was good.

And God blessed them, saying, Be fruitful, and multiply, and fill the waters in the seas, and let fowl multiply in the earth.

And the evening and the morning were the fifth day.

And God said, Let the earth bring forth the living creature after his kind, cattle, and creeping thing, and beast of the earth after his kind: and it was so. And God made the beast of the earth after his kind, and cattle after their kind, and every thing that creepeth upon the earth after his kind: and God saw that it was good.

Genesis 1:13-24

"...after his kind." *This eliminates evolution.*

If everything came from one source, then God would have only had to create one source. But notice, He said, *"Everything after his kind."* That means that cows don't produce horses, birds don't turn into crocodiles, crocodiles don't turn into rabbits, rabbits don't produce kangaroos, kangaroos don't have snakes, snakes don't make whales, whales don't make bees, bees don't make dinosaurs, dinosaurs don't make elephants, and elephants don't make mice.

There cannot be any such thing as evolution as we have been taught in school because evolution requires one common source, one origin, one thing, and out of that one thing everything else comes. God said that He created everything after its kind. That means that God started out with a horse, and from the time that the first horse came, horses are horses, and they don't turn into elephants.

The Creation of Mankind

And God said, Let us make man (not *men* plural, but *man* singular) **in our image, after our likeness: and let them** (man and woman) **have dominion over the fish of the sea, and over the fowl of the air, and over the cattle, and over all the earth, and over every creeping thing that creepeth upon the earth.**

So God created man in his own image, in the image of God created he him; male and female created he them.

And God blessed them, and God said unto them, Be fruitful, and multiply, and replenish the earth, and subdue it: and have dominion over the fish of the sea, and over the fowl of the air, and over every living thing that moveth upon the earth.

And God said, Behold, I have given you every herb bearing seed, which is upon the face of all the earth, and every tree, in the which is the fruit of a tree yielding seed; to you it shall be for meat.

And to every beast upon the earth, and to every fowl of the air, and to every thing that creepeth upon

the earth, wherein there is life, I have given every green herb for meat: and it was so.

And God saw every thing that he had made, and, behold, it was very good. And the evening and the morning were the sixth day.

Genesis 1:26-31

". . .and, behold, *it was very good*." That means that the man was good and the woman was good, and *they were separate.* There were no female men and no male females. Argue with God, if you like, but please don't argue with me. I did not create anything. I am only repeating what the Bible says.

God said that what He had made was good!

Therefore, anything other than what God made is not good. You have to be deaf, dumb, blind or dishonest not to see the implication of that. This would have to mean that gold is good, silver is good, diamonds are good, emeralds are good.

Notice that God made it all and gave it all to Adam. He did not give it to the devil's man. He gave it to the man He had created. The gold and the silver and everything that He had made, God gave to His man, Adam. That means that God must have wanted Adam to have it. If He wanted Adam to have it, then it must be all right for men to have it today.

The average Christian who does not accept the idea of material prosperity or who does not believe in having things, as such, did not get that idea from reading the Bible — he got it from some pulpit somewhere. If you read the Bible, you will know that prosperity is for you. This is only "Exhibit A." I am saving my best evidence for last. I have not yet finished presenting my case.

I believe that we have established beyond a shadow of a doubt that God made the material things of this earth which speak of wealth, such as gold, silver, diamonds, etc. Since God made these things, and since He considers them to be very good, then it must be all right for Fred, one of God's children, to have them. Since we have established that God created material things, who do you think He created them for — the devil and his crew? God did not make them for Himself, so He had to have made them for His man Adam, and we are the descendants of Adam.

Adam was a son of God. It is interesting to note that Abraham was not a son of God, but Adam was. Moses was not a son of God, but Adam was. Jacob was not a son of God, but Adam was — that is, until he sinned, then he lost (actually gave away) his sonship. This can be checked out in the Gospel in Luke, Chapter 3, beginning at verse 23:

> **And Jesus himself began to be about thirty years of age, being (as was supposed) the son of Joseph, which was the son of Heli.**

Then the passage continues to trace the genealogy of Joseph back to the beginning, which we read about in verse 38:

> **Which was the son of Enos, which was the son of Seth, which was the son of *Adam*, which *was the son of God*.**

When Adam sinned, he lost his sonship. He took himself out of the family of God. That was why redemption through Jesus had to come to mankind so that man could be brought back into the family of God by adoption. Adam was a natural son of God, but when He sinned he cut himself off, and everybody else.

To restore man to sonship with Himself, God established a divine "adoption agency" — Jesus Christ and the Holy Ghost. Through them, man can again become a son of God.

The Purpose of Wealth

I believe that I have established the fact that gold and other material possessions are good. Don't accuse me of being materialistic, because all I have done is expound on what the Bible says God has done. If anyone is going to be fair in leveling accusations, then he must call God materialistic, because He is the One Who created the gold, silver, diamonds, rubies, etc. All I am doing is talking about what God has created.

There are two ways for a Christian to get wealth: one is through the world's system (which is promoted by Satan), and the other is through God's system. Satan has a highly developed system, because he has a lot of willing customers. God has not had that many willing customers, because they have been deceived and conned into thinking that they are not supposed to have anything.

This kind of thinking has left the wealth of the world to fall into the hands of Satan so that he can control it and keep it out of the hands of the Body of Christ — which he has cleverly done. He has everything wrapped up. The majority of things are limited to his methodology.

Think about it: here is the Body of Christ whose Father owns the world, and we cannot go to any bank, major or minor, and borrow money to build a church. But the world can go and get money to build a liquor store, a hotel, an insurance building, an office building, or a burger joint. All things being equal, a person with proper credentials and collateral would have no problem getting money for any of these ventures. But Christians go through hell itself to get ten cents to build a church that is going to promote God. Why? Because Satan is behind the system, and he attempts to make everything difficult for the children of God. Yet, it is our Father Who owns the earth.

Isn't that something?

And because the devil has kept the wealth of the world out of our hands, we are at the mercy of the people who have the money. And the people who have the money are primarily Satan's people, or are in some way under the control of Satan's people. In other words, the ones who have the bulk of the wealth of this world are not the people who are interested in or committed to the proclamation of the Gospel of Jesus Christ. And so the churches just putter along, struggling to make ends met — *and it shouldn't be that way!*

It took me and my congregation 12 years to build a church, and not because there is a shortage of money. It was the system that hampered us. It does not take 12 years to build a hotel or a liquor store or a pool hall — you can get a loan for that. The only way to break the system is for us Christians to get hold of the wealth, and there is a way to do that.

We cannot get hold of the wealth by forsaking the spiritual aspect, because then it would be unstable wealth.

But we do have to get our hands on it. I intend to get my hands on it for the main purpose of helping the kingdom of God get the job done which God wants us to do.

The world needs to hear the Gospel!

It is only because of the influence of the Gospel in the western world that we have the kind of religious freedom that we enjoy in this nation. You and I do not have to be concerned about being killed or murdered because of our religious beliefs. But we will be persecuted! The Apostle Paul said, **. . .all that will live godly in Christ Jesus shall suffer persecution** (2 Tim. 3:12). This means that we will be talked about, criticized, ostracized, etc. But we don't have to be concerned about being burned at the stake or put into prison, as many Christians were in the days of the Early Church.

Some people have read about how things were in the early days of Christianity. They have read about how some believers were boiled in oil, or put into hot tar and their skin shaved off their bodies. They have heard about how in some countries around the world today Christians are being persecuted. Without realizing it, they have begun to believe that you have to be persecuted in order to serve God. I don't believe that at all. I don't find that anywhere in scripture. That is a fallacy. That is a deception of the devil to cause us to open the door and create the kind of atmosphere that will give him license to burn folks at the stake.

Things should get progressively better as the influence of the Gospel dulls the edge of the sword of the wicked one. Conditions ought to become better for us to live in this world.

Don't misunderstand me, I am not unaware that things will be bad at the end, but we are not at the end yet. In my humble opinion, we have a long way to go before we get there, based on what I see in the Word of God.

I believe 1 Timothy 2:1-3 gives good insight unto what we as Christians should be doing in regard to persecutions:

> **I exhort therefore, that, first of all, supplications, prayers, intercessions, and giving of thanks, be made for all men;**
>
> **For kings, and for all that are in authority....**

We don't have kings today in our nation, but we do have those who are in positions of authority, so this verse covers everybody: the president and vice-president, the cabinet, members of congress, senators, judges, police officers, firefighters — all those people who are in public office, all those who govern us or who make decisions that affect our lives.

> **...that we may lead a quiet and peaceable life** (not a burning-at-the-stake or a fed-to-the-lions type of life) **in all godliness and honesty.**

Why?

> **For this is good and acceptable in the sight of God our Saviour.**
>
> **I Timothy 2:4**

According to the Bible, a peaceable life is good and acceptable in the sight of God. It is acceptable to God for us to live in peace. But we are not going to have peace if we don't first do what Paul exhorts us to do here in this passage: pray for all who are in authority.

Thank God that He was able to get the attention of a few folks to establish this nation in which people have a right to practice their religious beliefs. So don't go around looking for persecution. There is nothing intrinsically valuable in being persecuted. Jesus simply mentioned that persecution "goes with the territory." It is a natural result of serving Him. He was persecuted, and we will be too, because we belong to Him. We will never be able to completely rid ourselves of some form of persecution, unless we get rid of Satan, because he is the one who is behind it all. But it ought to be controlled persecution. We ought to be on such a plane of spirituality and have created such an environment of peace that the persecution will be minimal.

5

It Is the Lord
That Giveth Thee Wealth

I believe that it has been firmly established in preceding chapters that God's covenant (or agreement) with us, which He made through His Son Jesus Christ, promises us abundant life. The word *"abundant"* means "more than enough."

But again, what is this abundance for? It is so we will be able to give, to make what we have available to God for His work.

Right now you may be thinking: "Well, I don't know about making anything available to God. I am having a hard enough time just paying my bills."

That is exactly the object of the system, that is what has kept you trying to make it, trying to survive. If you ever rise above the survival status and get to the point where you are abundantly supplied in every area of your life so that you do not have to think about your own needs, then you will be able to become sensitive to the leading of the Spirit of God and can become a channel of blessing to others.

All of the material blessings that we receive from God have to come to us through someone!

77

When you get to the place where you don't have to be concerned about your own needs, you can have more time to think about other people's needs — more time to think about God!

Answers Attract Others

Think about this: What made Jesus so attractive to those among whom He walked almost 2,000 years ago? He was probably attractive to them because He was sick all the time. It was His illness that drew other sick people to Him for healing, because He was always in the hospital Himself. His weakness and disease is what drew their attention to Him.

No!

You mean that sick people didn't come to Jesus because they felt He could sympathize with their condition because He Himself was sick just as they were?

No!

The Church world never thinks about this point: What drew people to Jesus? He operated completely outside the religious establishment of His day. By all standards, because of His unorthodox life, He should not have had anyone following Him. No one should have listened to Him because He operated outside the synagogue system. Yet He had people following Him by the thousands.

Why?

What was it about Jesus that attracted people to Him? Could it have been that they knew He could feed 5,000 with a few loaves and a couple of fish? Could it have been that He could provide food for hungry people, healing for sick people, relief for hurting people? Was that it?

You have to get a person's attention before you can preach the Gospel to him. It is hard to talk to a person about getting saved when he is hurting, blind with pain. You have to do something to ease his suffering before he is ready or even able to listen.

Give a hungry man something to eat, give a hurting man something to take away his pain, and then tell me that he won't listen to what you have to say! He will want to know what you are saying then.

"What have You got going, Jesus? Tell me more!"

You may have to help that person first. How are you going to do that if you don't have the ability to do it? Sometimes Christians think all they have to do is stand on the corner and preach about Jesus. But Jesus is about meeting people's needs. Yes, spiritual needs come *first*, but sometimes in order to get to the first item, we have to do some other things to get a needy person's attention.

When you look as if your own needs are not met, who is going to have any confidence to believe that you can do anything for him? You have no credibility. Who is going to listen to a loser?

Just imagine the scene: There you are, sitting on the street corner saying, "Now, I am going to tell all you people how to keep your cars and homes; I am going to show you how to keep folks from repossessing your house and car." And just about that time, your creditors drive up in front of your own house to jack up your car and foreclose on your home, nailing it shut. If you were one of those people on the street, would you listen to someone like you?

God's Purpose in Giving Us Power to Get Wealth

But thou shalt remember *the Lord thy God*: for it is he that *giveth thee power to get wealth,* that he may *establish his covenant* which he sware unto thy fathers, as it is this day.

Deuteronomy 8:18

Notice that this verse does not say, "...for it is he that giveth thee wealth." Wouldn't that be easier? We could cut out some of these steps if God would just say, "I am the Lord Who gives you wealth." But He does not say that! He says that He gives us the *power* to get wealth!

Again, why? For what purpose are we to get wealth?

To establish the covenant!

What is the covenant? It is God's promise to provide us with *abundant* life!

This is what is pleasing in the sight of God, and it is what is going to attract other people.

Let's look at that verse again: "But thou shalt remember the Lord thy God: for it is he that giveth thee power to get wealth..." (remember that "wealth' means "goods, riches, substance") "...that *he may establish his covenant which he sware unto thy fathers,* as it is this day."

Apparently, according to this scripture, the covenant cannot be established or completed without wealth.

I like to add words every once in a while; it helps to make the meaning a little clearer. Notice where this verse says, "...for it is he that giveth thee power to get wealth, that he may establish his covenant...." Drop the word "so" right in between the words "wealth" and "that." Then the verse would read like this: "...for it is he that giveth thee power to get wealth, *so* that he may establish his covenant...."

In other words, there is a purpose for the wealth. The wealth is not for wealth's sake, but the wealth is given *"so that."* That is important to understand. "So that" what? "...so that he may establish his covenant which *he* sware...." The "he" refers to God.

The implication here is that God cannot establish His covenant without our cooperation. God is under our control in our individual lives. He gives us power to get wealth so that He may establish His covenant with us forever.

God Depends Upon Us

God is unlimited. But based on the way He has designed the system to work, He is limited relative to His establishing His covenant in us, because He cannot do it without us.

Yes, God can do anything, by virtue of the fact that He is God, and He has the power, but He cannot do anything that would violate His Word, because it is forever settled in heaven. (Ps. 119:89.) If God were to violate His own Word, that would make Him like man instead of God, because men violate their word all the time. But God cannot violate His Word without reducing Himself to the level of a mere human being.

You will not find these particular words in the Bible, but the principle is there: God's covenant is for us to have "life, liberty and the pursuit of happiness." What is the "life, liberty and the pursuit of happiness" to which we are entitled?

Satan will try to play tricks with your mind, and you will begin to think about people you know of in the world who have, or appear to have, what we have mistakenly thought was happiness — because they have a lot of money. Money is a part of wealth, but a person can have millions of dollars and still be poor — poor in health, poor in peace of mind and heart, poor in friendships.

Who are your real friends? How do you know that your best friend really loves you and not your money? True wealth encompasses more than just material riches.

I remember several years ago I read an article in a local newspaper about one of the richest men in the world. I believe it said that he had been married three or four times. So apparently all that money he possessed had not made him happy or provided him a totally satisfied life.

A lot of people think that if they could just get enough money they would be happy.

But that is not necessarily true!

From what I have read in the Word, I believe there is a place in God where you and I can have it all —

the wealth and the peace of mind that should go with it, along with the wisdom of God to be able to live with that wealth and deal with it wisely, so that it becomes the means to an end and not the end in itself. The true wealth that God gives — true prosperity — will have everything "going for it" and with it.

Notice what this verse says: "...for it is he that giveth thee power to *get* wealth...." That would have to mean that the wealth is already here — that the wealth is not in God's hands or under His control, because if it were, why wouldn't He give it to His children? But the Bible says that God gives us the *power* to *get* wealth. Therefore, whether we get it or not is up to us. It is our duty and responsibility to see that the acquisition of wealth does not become the end of our existence. There is no problem with this because Philippians 4:13 tells us that we can do all things through Christ Who strengthens us.

The Purpose of Wealth

Remember, the purpose of wealth is *to establish the covenant.*

What is included in the covenant?

Abundant life and everything that goes with it!

This is talking about doing the will of God, about preaching the Gospel, about proclaiming the Word of God. It is talking about everything that has to do with making life what it ought to be. It means happiness, health, prosperity in every way and in every area of our lives: our marriage, our children, our body, our business, our work, our ministry.

Many times people cannot achieve success in life because they have so many "hang ups." They can never get to the point of accomplishment because there are all these things that hang them up along the way: "Well, I cannot do that because...." "I cannot have this because...." "Christians are not supposed to do that because...." "God doesn't want us to have this because...." "The Church says that we can't...."

All these are "hang ups" and roadblocks!

Before you and I can achieve God's best for our lives, we have got to get rid of all the blocks that hinder us.

You have to have a tool to get a job done — whatever that tool might be. It could be a typewriter in your business; it could be a wrench, a screwdriver, a hammer or a slide rule. It could be anything. This may sound strange, but God has a tool — and that tool is you and me. In other words, we are God's tools.

God is limited by His tools in the same way that a craftsman is limited by the quality of his equipment. A secretary is absolutely powerless if she has a typewriter that has no ribbon in it. I don't want a surgeon operating on me with a hammer and a chisel; if he does not have the proper tools and equipment, he is severely hampered.

By the same token, God is hampered if He does not have the proper tools. We are God's chest of tools. One of us may be a screwdriver, one of us may be a wrench, one of us may be a hammer, one may be a saw, and so on. God cannot fix anything the way it needs to be repaired if His tools are not working properly!

You and I must get into a position where we can function effectively as tools in the hands of God. We must be about His business, accomplishing His will, not our own!

In the process of doing God's will, all of our own will can be taken care of. This is the unique and beautiful thing about God's "set up." While you and I are busy doing His will, our will is being taken care of. When we fulfill His desire, our desire is seen to. This is just one of the "fringe benefits" that go along with serving God.

But if we are not functioning correctly, then God is going to be limited in what He can do — only because that is the way He has designed the system.

Prosperity Pleases God

Let them shout for joy, and be glad, that favour my righteous cause: yea, let them say continually, Let *the Lord* be magnified, which *hath pleasure in the prosperity of his servant.*

Psalm 35:27

If God has pleasure in our prosperity, He must have displeasure in our poverty. The opposite of pleasure is displeasure. The opposite of prosperity is poverty.

If God has pleasure in the prosperity of His *servant*, what must He have in the prosperity of His *child*? If you have been born again, then you are not a servant of God, *you are a child of God!*

85

Removing the Roadblocks on the Road to Prosperity

I have said that sometimes there are different roadblocks in the Christian life. They often come because of association, observation and teaching. There are certain things that Satan will use to block the minds of God's people.

There are some people who cannot believe certain things about God, only because they have been exposed to a particular persuasion all their lives. They cannot believe that God wants them to be well. There are others who cannot bring themselves to believe that God wants them to be healed. Still others have a hard time believing that God wants them to be prosperous.

Many times people have been taught and conditioned to think that they are supposed to be poor or sick — that God is somehow pleased with or glorifed by their distress.

"I am suffering for the Lord," they say.

No, they are not "suffering for the Lord"! They are suffering because they are ignorant — ignorant of God's Word.

Such people are sincere about their beliefs. They are not playing games. They are committed to the proposition that they are supposed to be poor or sick "for the glory of God" — that somehow God gets something out of their pain and suffering.

In other words, they believe that if they can "keep a stiff upper lip" through it all, and never renounce God, that somehow the Lord will get pleasure or glory out of their predicament. There are some people who believe this so strongly that they cannot be talked to about it. They are totally closed-minded on this subject. It is pathetic and so sad to see them being cheated out of all that God wants them to have — yet they don't even realize it. All their beliefs have come about because of association, observation and teaching which has come from wrong thinkers and wrong thinking. But until these roadblocks are removed, these people will never be able to move into the fullness of the things of God.

6

God Shall Supply All Your Need

At the time the book of Philippians was written, the Apostle Paul was incarcerated in a prison in Rome. Many of the churches he had established, or been involved with in some way, had sent personal items to him to minister to his physical needs during his imprisonment. They were concerned about him, because they loved him and appreciated his ministry to them.

In response to their concern and generosity, Paul writes:

> But I rejoiced in the Lord greatly, that now at the last your care of me hath flourished again; wherein ye were also careful, but ye lacked opportunity.
>
> Philippians 4:10

In other words, Paul is saying, "You wanted to help me, but you didn't have the opportunity or the chance to do so."

"...for I have learned..."

> Not that I speak in respect of want: for *I have learned*, in whatsoever state I am, therewith to be content.
>
> Philippians 4:11

Notice that Paul writes: "I have *learned....*"

89

The way you learn is a combination of precept and example. In other words, you can learn by the words that you are taught, but then what you are taught should be augmented by what you experience. When this is the case, the experience will validate and confirm beyond any doubt what you have learned from the book. What you learn from a book is somebody else's experience, which may be true, but the Word will never become *rhema* (alive) to you until you experience it for yourself.

What happens with so many people is that they hear the Word of God taught, and they rejoice in it. It sounds great and wonderful, but they never take enough time to experience the Word for themselves. They may do it for a while, but because what they are believing for does not manifest itself instantly, because results are not immediately forthcoming, they say, "Ah, that stuff doesn't work." They don't realize that in most cases time has to pass before the manifestation occurs.

You have to allow time to pass before you can experience a return on your effort. And sometimes it's not until you have gone through something experientially, over and over again, that it becomes real to you.

I'm not necessarily speaking of something negative — I am talking about the normal process of learning which all of us human beings go through in our daily lives.

It's like when you learn how to drive a car. You are sort of shaky at first, and you are very careful because you're nervous. After all, this is a big thing. Automobiles are whizzing past you and trucks are going by; there are buses and pedestrian traffic all around, and dogs and kids are running across the street ahead of you. You have learned all the proper procedures by studying the book, and now you are having an actual experience of driving. But it's not until after you have driven a while that driving becomes second nature to you.

Eventually it becomes quite natural for you to drive, but at first it is very traumatic to get behind the wheel. The more you drive, the more proficient you become at driving. The more accustomed to driving you become, the easier it gets.

It's the same way with just about every experience of life that we go through. Understand that I am mainly addressing the positive side of learning. I'm not talking about going through some hellish experience which you have to experience 99 times before you finally get the message. You don't need to go through hellish experiences but one time — and really not even once!

If all of us were smart and learned from other people's experiences, in addition to learning, of course, by instruction from the Word of God, then none of us would need to go through any hellish times at all. But unfortunately, this is not the case. Consequently, some people must go through some unhappy experiences over and over because they will not learn any other way. But having gone through a tragedy, surely we need not repeat it again and again before learning our lesson.

Paul says that he has learned. The way he learned was by personal experience based upon and confirmed by the Word of God.

"...to be content"

"...I have learned, in whatsoever state I am, therewith *to be content.*"

Now the Greek word translated "content" here in this verse is very interesting. It literally means "to be self-sufficient." It means "to be adequate in oneself." It means "needing no assistance."

When we use the word "content," many times it carries the connotation of: "Well, I don't have what I really want, but I'll just *content* myself with what I have. I really want to live up on the top of the hill in a mansion, but I'll just be *content* to live down here by the riverside in this shotgun shack. I'll drive this horse and buggy; at least it gets me from point A to point B. I'm not really satisfied with this mode of transportation, this is not what I ultimately desire, I would really like to have a Rolls Royce, but I'll just *content* myself with it."

This word "content" doesn't mean that at all. What it means is: "I am self-sufficient. I am adequate in myself. I need no assistance."

If I am self-sufficient, if I am adequate in myself, if I have no need of assistance, then I am content.

Now this self-sufficiency, this adequacy, this lack of need of assistance is all based upon the fact that we have God as our source. This is what Paul is alluding to here in this passage. He is not saying that he is self-sufficient, adequate, without need of assistance — in himself. What he is saying is: "I am self-sufficient in the Greater One Who is in me. I am adequate, I need no assistance, because the Greater One abides within.

I have the best helper anyone could possibly ask for. I have assistance that is beyond the realm of human understanding. I have supernatural assistance by the Holy Spirit."

Then he goes on to elaborate on the cause of this sense of contentment which he enjoys.

Knowing How To Live Victoriously in Every Circumstance of Life

I know both how to be abased, and I know how to abound: every where and in all things I am instructed (by experience) **both to be full and to be hungry, both to abound and to suffer** (put up with) **need.**

I can do all things through Christ which strengtheneth me.

Philippians 4:12,13

In this passage Paul lists the different states that one could find himself in, and no doubt these are the ones that he had come through successfully in his life and ministry. He says: "I know both how to be abased (in other words, how to be put down), *and how to abound* (how to be above). . . ." Then he points out that he has learned from experience how to be full and to be hungry, how to abound and how to put up with need.

But notice something very carefully here, because if you don't, you could fall into a trap. Paul is not saying that we have to be abased. He is not saying that we have to abound. He is not saying that we have to be full. He is not saying that we have to be hungry. He is not saying that we have to suffer need or go with our needs unmet.

93

Paul is not saying any of these things at all. What he is saying is: "I, Paul, have learned how to go through all these things." He never said that he was in them now, and he never said that they were the goals of his life or ours: to suffer want, to be in need, or to live with unmet needs. He is simply saying that he has learned, by virtue of his personal experience of going though these things, how to deal with all of them.

What Paul is saying to us here in this passage is: "If the situation necessitated that I go with my needs unmet, I could do so, because I can do all things through Christ Who gives me the strength to face life and to live victoriously in spite of circumstances."

While Paul is not telling us to live in want, with our needs unmet, we can be like him and we can survive whatever comes, because we can do it all through Christ, Who gives us the strength to do anything and everything.

Follow Christ, Not Men

Most people can't do that. They would be totally wiped out if a negative situation arose against them. They would go to pieces and fall completely apart.

For example, I know some people who can't live the Christian life in line with the Word of God because of watching other Christians. Instead of taking their cue from the Word of God, they attempt to follow other believers. They attempt to measure Christianity by the actions of other people.

That's the worst trap we could ever fall into. You and I are never told to follow other Christians. We are only encouraged to follow other people *as they follow*

Christ. But suppose they are not following Christ to the letter of the Word. We will never know whether they are or not until we ourselves know the Word sufficiently well enough to judge their actions.

Friend, if I had become a Christian and a minister of the Gospel because I had been watching other believers and preachers, I would have quit 99 years ago. Based on the garbage that I have seen, and the stuff that I have had to put up with from other Christians and ministers, I would have given up ages ago. But Jesus has never failed me, and He will never fail you — if you will keep your eyes on Him through the application of His Word to your life.

It is a fool's choice to follow other Christians and then to throw up the actions of other believers as an excuse for not doing what is right.

The Bible says that Jesus has left us an example. (1 Pet. 2:21.) We are told that we are to follow His example.

As a Christain you are not supposed to take me as your example. Now I ought to live right, but you are a fool if you choose to follow me — of myself. You can safely follow me only as long as I follow Christ. You can see an example of Jesus lived out in human life and in human flesh by following me, but still you are not going to know whether I am doing what Jesus said to do or not unless you know for yourself what the Word says.

A lot of Christians are lazy. They don't want to take the time to study the Word. They don't want to devote themselves to serious Bible study, to spend the time it takes to research it and discover what it really says about a particular subject. It is so much easier to just take somebody else's word. That's the reason why, when I teach the Bible, I have people look at their own Bibles. I'm interested in people finding out for themselves what the Bible says.

A Christian should be following Christ and not other Christians. And I'll tell you right now, don't think that when you come to stand before God you can use that old alibi that you were misled by me or anybody else. He's not going to go for it!

Can you imagine what the Lord will say to anyone standing before Him claiming: "Well, Lord, I would have done Your will, but Fred Price didn't...."

"Wait. Who's Fred Price? What does he have to do with you?"

You will have to stand before God for yourself, just as I will have to stand before Him for myself. That's why I don't let anybody — my wife and children included — hinder me from doing what I know is right to do. They can do whatever they please. I hope they pray and read the Bible. I encourage them to pray. I encourage them to read the Word. But if they stop praying and reading the Bible, that's their problem — not mine. I know what to do, and I don't have any excuse for not doing it. I'm going to have to answer to God for myself for what I do and fail to do.

God Is Our Source

Paul tells us that he had learned how to be self-sufficient in every one of the situations of life because God was his source.

You can learn how to be self-sufficient by growing up spiritually, because 99 people out of a 100 start out the Christian life already whipped, defeated, sick, poor, scared — or whatever. You didn't come into Christ already spiritually mature, did you? The majority of us came in all messed up. In fact, the reason most of us came to Him in the first place was because we were messed up and couldn't do anything for ourselves. He was the only One Who would have us. Our family had given up on us. Our relatives had kicked us out. Our friends had stopped associating with us. Even the dog had started barking at us. Nobody would have us but God. We all came to Jesus with our bags full of "mess ups."

Even though you may have started out that way, you can grow up — you can mature in Christ. As you go through the various experiences of life, you ought to learn something from each of them. At least you ought to learn that you do not have to go through that same thing again. You learn how to overcome by overcoming. You learn how to win by winning. You never learn how to overcome by failing; you never learn how to win by losing.

God is our source. Even if the economy folds up, we don't have to fold up. In years gone by, our nation went through the Great Depression. There were many people who were millionaires, who had everything they owned invested in the stock market. When the market fell through, they ended up killing themselves. They couldn't take it; they couldn't handle it.

But Paul tells us Christians that we can do all things through Christ. We don't have to fall apart or go to pieces, because God is our source and Christ is always there to strengthen us.

It is amazing to me how many Christians want instant success. Success doesn't come instantly. In anything worthwhile, there is a time factor involved.

God is our source, but even He takes time.

Blessed to Become a Blessing

Notwithstanding ye have well done, that ye did communicate with my affliction.

Now ye Philippians know also, that in the beginning of the gospel, when I departed from Macedonia, no church communicated with me as concerning giving and receiving, but ye only.

For even in Thessalonica ye sent once and again unto my necessity.

Not because I desire a gift: but I desire fruit that may abound to your account.

Philippians 4:14-17

"...ye did communicate with my *affliction.*" Literally, the word "affliction" means "tribulation." Paul is speaking here about his having to be confined to prison.

"Not because I desire a gift: but I desire *fruit that may abound to your account.*" In my opinion, that ought to be the watchword of the ministry. It also ought to be the watchword to you as an individual Christian, that fruit may abound to *your* account.

This is the purpose of the teaching of the Word, so that you will be the recipient of the truth, and that you, by and through the truth, will be blessed.

Blessed to become a blessing.

But you cannot be a blessing until you are blessed yourself. You can't give what you don't have, and you have to get it in order to have it.

"...my God shall supply all your need..."

But I have all, and abound: I am full, having received of Epaphroditus the things which were sent from you, an odour of a sweet smell, a sacrifice acceptable, wellpleasing to God.

But my God shall supply all your need according to his riches in glory by Christ Jesus.

Philippians 4:18,19

The truth that is stated in verse 19 needs to be assimilated into our thinking and into our spirits. Notice what Paul says: "...*my God shall supply all your need*...."

Notice that he does not say that God will supply all our "needs," but that He will supply our all "*need*." That covers everything, all the time, at one time. Whatever you and I need, our God will supply.

"...according to his riches in glory..."

How does God supply all our need?

"...*according to his* riches in glory...."

Not according to our poverty. Not according to our empty wallet, not according to our empty meal barrel, and not according to our empty refrigerator.

Sometimes what happens is that when people get to a point of need, they start looking at the natural and try to figure out how God is going to meet their need.

Then when they can't figure it out, they try to help God out — and that's when they get into trouble.

Don't ever start doing something on your own because you can't figure out how God is going to meet your need.

My wife and I have gone through many things over the years of our walking together in the Word. Many times there was no way we could figure out how God was going to meet our desperate need. Now as we look back, we see that it was all taken care of. It's done and over, and God did it.

"...by Christ Jesus."

How do God's riches in glory come to us?

"...by Christ Jesus."

It is *through Christ* that we receive God's riches to meet all of our need.

In verse 13, Paul states: "I can do all things through Christ which strengtheneth me." God can do all things through Christ. And He has said that He will supply all our need by Christ Jesus.

But We Have a Part To Play

But the way that we receive God's provision is to follow the directives of His Word. It's a cyclical process. And everyone in the cycle has a part to play in it. If any one person in the cycle does not play his part, the cycle breaks down. God has a part to play, Christ has a part to play, the Holy Spirit has a part to play, and you and I have a part to play. We know that God,

Christ, and the Holy Spirit are not going to fail to do their part, so that leaves us — you and me.

A chain is only as strong as its weakest link. It took me many years to figure that statement out. I later learned that it means that the strength of the entire chain is dependent upon the strength of its weakest link. The rest of the chain is only as strong as its weakest link because when that link breaks, the whole chain is broken. Whatever amount of pressure that weakest link can withstand determines the strength of the entire length.

God the Father, Jesus, the Holy Spirit and you and I are the four links. We are the weakest link of that chain or cycle. If we don't do our part, then the Father, Jesus, and the Holy Spirit are hindered from doing their part. Each of us has our individual part to play.

This verse says that God shall supply all of our need according to His riches in glory by Christ Jesus. But that statement cannot be lifted out of the context of the entire Bible. Sometimes we quote it to make a point that God will always meet our needs, but in reality that statement is related to everything else in the Bible that God tells us to do in order to prosper.

If you and I don't do what the Bible tells us to do, then God is not going to be able to supply our need according to His riches in glory by Christ Jesus.

The Word of God is also the Word of Christ, and the Word tells us what to do. If we don't do what it tells us, then we have broken the link in the chain, and God cannot meet our need.

For example, the Word of God says to give and it shall be given to us. If we do not give, then it shall not be given to us. There is no way something we have not given can be multiplied back to us. I don't see why people can't see that. It works the same way in the world. It's amazing how some people can see this principle in operation in the world, but have such a problem with it in the Bible.

It's interesting that people can take $10,000 and put it into a T-bill account, knowing full well that in order to receive maximum benefit (and not be penalized) they have to leave it there for the full term. Most people have no problem with that concept. Yet many of these same people expect God to respond yesterday. They just started investing in the Lord's work today, but they want a return yesterday. They can wait six months for a T-bill to mature, and have no problem understanding the necessity for that waiting period, but they can't understand why God's promised return takes so long.

These people can spend four years going to college to get a degree, and have no problem with that. They don't cry or faint or pitch a fit or beat down the dean's office door, crying: "I don't know why I can't get my bachelor's degree. I've been going to class here for six whole months; why won't you give me my degree?"

Do you know why? Because the academic system is based on a principle. All things being equal, it takes approximately four years of study to earn a bachelor's degree. People will study and work and wait patiently four years to receive their degree, but they won't wait four days to give the Word of God time to mature in their lives. They want it to "pay off" yesterday. They will wait six months for a T-bill to come to maturity, but they won't wait six hours for God to answer their prayers.

The bank has their $10,000. They won't see it again for six months. Why didn't they put that amount into the Church? Why didn't they invest that money in the Lord's work? And then give Him six months to provide them a return on their investment? No, they put their offering in on Sunday morning and expect a return on the following Saturday. When that expected return doesn't materialize immediately, they are ready to say, "Ah, that stuff doesn't work."

If this describes the way you operate, I have something to say to you: "You dishonest rascal, *it will work if you work it!*"

Everything is governed by principles — by laws — and you have to put them into action, and then give them time to work.

God's Word Works!

My God shall supply all your need!

I can say this not only from the standpoint of Philippians 4:19, but also from the standpoint of personal experience.

God will supply your need. But you have to be willing to make a commitment to the Lord.

Sometimes people look at me and see the things that I have, from the standpoint of what the world calls success, and they think that I am supposed to give them something. I used to be that way too. I used to be a "cry baby," a beggar, a borrower. I begged and borrowed all the time because I never had enough. I would borrow from anybody who would loan me money. Then I'd be up to my neck trying to pay it back.

Once I discovered that God's Word works (my wife can verify this statement), I never asked anybody for anything or borrowed any more money to take care of my personal matters. In fact, I stopped telling anybody about my finanical situation. Whereas before I used to cry all the time and tell anybody who would listen: "Have I told you about my latest problem? The canary swallowed the cat this morning!"

However, once I found out about the Word, I had a different attitude about how to handle my finances. My wife and I agreed together and made a quality decision that we were going with the Word — that it was going to work for us, that it was going to produce the abundant life for us. We had to sacrifice at first. We had to go without. Many people don't want to make a sacrifice or go without. We did so because that's what it took to get us to where we wanted to be.

Now we don't go without any more, but we didn't get to that place overnight.

Somewhere along the way you have to make a commitment, and then honor that commitment in your own life; otherwise, you will never know the reality of God's Word for yourself.

Nobody can tell me that the Word of God doesn't work. Nobody — but *nobody* — can tell me that the Word will not do what God says it will do.

It works!

But It Must Be Put into Action!

But you have to be willing to make the commitment, and it may cost you something in the beginning. But you have to be determined to work the Word.

It cost us. We went without a lot of things because we were seeking a higher goal. We saw what life could be like, and we made a commitment to reach our goal. Now we're blessed coming and going — just as God said we would be — just as the psalmist wrote:

> Blessed is the man that walketh not in the counsel of the ungodly, nor standeth in the way of sinners, nor sitteth in the seat of the scornful.
>
> But his delight is in the law (the Word) of the Lord; and in his law (Word) doth he meditate day and night.
>
> And he shall be like a tree planted by the rivers of water, that bringeth forth his fruit in his season; his leaf also shall not wither; and whatsoever he doeth shall prosper.
>
> **Psalm 1:1-3**

"...and *in his law doth he meditate day and night*." Not once a month, not just at Christmas or Easter, New Year's Day or Groundhog Day, but *"day and night"* — *night and day!*

"...and *whatsover he doeth shall prosper*." Whatsoever. Whatsoever. "Whatsoever" means your marriage relationship, your family, your children, your business, your ministry. It means your job, your health — it means *everything!*

But it won't prosper until you start doing what the Word says.

It took me 17 years to get into the mess I was in. I worked at it for 17 years. I had it down to a science. When the end of the seventeenth year came, I was so fouled up, so messed up, so strung out, so hung up financially, economically, and physically, that I was nothing but a wreck going some place to happen.

But my wife and I came out of that mess in a lot less then 17 years. We have been out of it for a number of years now, but it took some time. Now we can be a blessing. Not only are we blessed, but we can be a blessing to others — and that is the "bottom line."

However, I am careful about who I am a blessing to. I am not going to bless some lazy, good-for-nothing somebody who doesn't want to take the time or make the effort to make whatever commitment that is necessary in order to ultimately succeed. I wouldn't give a person like that a dime. I wouldn't even give him the time of day, because he can do just as I did — but he refuses.

You too can make the same commitment I made. When I see somebody making that commitment — when I see somebody putting forth effort, I will help him (as I am led to do so). I will give him something. I am not going to give it to some lazy rascal who is just sitting around with his hand out, saying, "My name is Jimmy, I'll take all you gimme."

No!

I'll say it a million times, until Jesus comes: *You have to put the Word into operation or it won't work for you!*

It takes dedication. It takes discipline. It takes staying with it until it manifests.

Prosperity is, and always has been, for the Christian.

But it has to be on *God's terms* — *and God's terms are outlined in His Word.*

Other Books by Fred Price

Practical Suggestions
for Successful Ministry

Prosperity on God's Terms

Concerning Them Which Are Asleep

Marriage and the Family
Practical Insight for Family Living

High Finance
God's Financial Plan
Tithes and Offerings

Homosexuality
State of Mind or State of Birth?

Living in the Realm of the Spirit

Is Healing for All?

How Faith Works
(also available in Spanish)

How To Obtain Strong Faith
Six Principles

The Holy Spirit — The Missing Ingredient

Faith, Foolishness, or Presumption?

Thank God for Everything?

The Origin of Satan

Name It and Claim It

How To Believe God for a Mate

Now Faith Is

HARRISON HOUSE
P.O. Box 35035 • Tulsa, OK 74153

In Canada contact:: Word Alive • P.O. Box 284
Niverville, Manitoba • CANADA ROA 1EO

For a complete list of tapes and books by Fred Price, or to receive his quarterly publication, *Ever Increasing Faith Messenger*, write:

Crenshaw Christian Center
P.O. Box 90000
Los Angeles, California 90009
or call: Area code 213/758-3777